# The Costs of Crime and Justice

Politicians and pundits frequently talk about the costs of crime to society, but few ever define their terms or clarify their statistics. So how does a society measure economic loss owing to criminal activity?

In *The Costs of Crime and Justice*, Mark A. Cohen presents a comprehensive view of the financial setbacks of criminal behavior. Victims of crime might incur medical costs, lost wages, and property damage; while for some crimes pain, suffering, and reduced quality of life suffered by victims far exceed any physical damage. The government also incurs costs as the provider of mental health services, police, courts, and prisons.

Cohen argues that understanding the costs of crime can lead to important insights and policy conclusions—both in terms of criminal justice policy and in terms of other social ills that compete with crime for government funding. This book systematically discusses the numerous methodological approaches and tallies up what is known about the costs of crime.

A must-read for anyone involved in criminal justice or public policy, *The Costs of Crime and Justice* consolidates the diverse research in this area but also makes one of the most valuable contributions to date to the study of the economics of criminal behavior.

**Mark A. Cohen** holds the Justin Potter Chair in Competitive American Business and is Senior Associate Dean at the Owen Graduate School of Management, Vanderbilt University. He is also a Visiting Professor of Criminal Justice Economics at the University of York (U.K.). He is the author of more than 50 books and journal articles on crime and economics.

# The Costs of Crime and Justice

Mark A. Cohen

Routledge
Taylor & Francis Group

LONDON AND NEW YORK

First published 2005
by Routledge
2 Park Square, Milton Park, Abingdon, Oxon OX14 4RN

Simultaneously published in the USA and Canada
by Routledge
270 Madison Ave, New York, NY 10016

*Routledge is an imprint of the Taylor & Francis Group*

Typeset in Sabon by The Running Head Limited, Cambridge
Printed and bound in Great Britain by T J International Ltd,
Padstow, Cornwall

*British Library Cataloguing in Publication Data*
A catalogue record for this book is available from the British Library

*Library of Congress Cataloging in Publication Data*
A catalog record for this book has been requested

ISBN 0–415–70072–8 (hbk)
ISBN 0–415–70073–6 (pbk)

To Robin—who taught me to value what is most important in life . . .

# Contents

# Tables and figure

## Tables

## Figure

# Preface

This book is a culmination of 18 years of sporadic journeys into estimating the costs of crime and justice. My travels began rather serendipitously as I never studied crime in college or graduate school. I am an economist—trained to analyze the allocation of resources in society. My dissertation was concerned with the optimal enforcement policy to reduce oil spills—and I adapted the Gary Becker (1968) model of the economics of crime to analyze government penalties and enforcement policies designed to prevent oil spills from tankers and to conduct a benefit–cost analysis of the government's policy (Cohen, 1986 and 1987). In 1985, when the newly established United States Sentencing Commission was in the process of being formed, I received a phone call from Professor Michael Block at the University of Arizona. Professor Block was one of the few economists who specialized in analyzing crime issues. He had just been appointed by President Reagan to be a Commissioner of the new Sentencing Commission and was looking for a young economist who knew something about the economics of crime. I told him that I was not his man, since I knew nothing about crime. That did not seem to matter to him. I suspect he hired me because he could not find any other newly minted Ph.D. economist who was knowledgeable in this area. Thus my journey began.

The first few days on the job were fascinating. I was literally the first staff member to arrive at the Commission other than a few secretaries. I sat around the table with eight Commissioners—including several judges—one of whom, Stephen Breyer, would later be appointed to the Supreme Court. The Commissioners turned to me and asked if I could do some research and brief them on (a) how social scientists have ranked the severity of crime, and (b) what is known about the factors judges use to sentence offenders. While I worked on both issues over the next several months, the first question was most intriguing. I found a vast literature beginning with Sellin and Wolfgang's (1966) path-breaking public perception surveys used to rank crime severity. While these methods are valuable—and have withstood the test of time—the economist in me asked if there was a more objective way to rank crime severity—the actual harm caused by crime. Thus I began to look for any study that placed dollar values on crime—with the ultimate goal of being able to conduct benefit–cost analyses.

What I found was a dearth of information on the costs of crime and—more importantly—a serious misuse of the data that was available. The most stark example (discussed further in Chapter 5) is an excellent study, conducted by James Austin (1986), that analyzed an Illinois early-release program and its impact on recidivism and costs. He found that the reduced prison costs (i.e. savings to taxpayers) more than offset the cost associated with the slight increase in crimes committed by recidivists. However, the "costs" of higher crimes that Austin used were those published by the National Institute of Justice—they only included the "out-of-pocket" costs such as medical costs and damaged property. It is hard to fault Austin for using these numbers—they were all that was available at the time. However, the result was a dramatic reversal of policy recommendations. The cost of a rape was assumed to be only about $350 in his study. Thus if a prisoner was let out early and committed a rape while he otherwise would have been in prison the "cost" of that failure was estimated to be $350 plus some additional criminal justice processing fees. From these data, Austin (1986) concluded that the Illinois early-release program was a good one that saved money.

It was the Austin study that led me to what I would almost admit was a crusade. It was clear that benefit–cost analyses would be (and should be) conducted in the future in the criminal justice policy arena. Yet the only numbers available for the "benefits" of crime reductions (or the "costs" of crime) were woefully inadequate. It was beyond embarrassing to see a benefit–cost analysis that valued a rape at $350. I began to search for a better approach to estimating the cost of crime. While methods used in the environmental economics literature existed, they were still in their infancy at the time, required a considerable amount of time and money to implement, and would take years before any consensus on their calculation and implementation could be developed. Later, in Chapter 2, we will explore those approaches—which have developed further and which are now beginning to be applied to criminal justice issues as well. In the interim, however, an idea came to Professor Phil Cook from Duke University, one of the best-known economists who has written on the economics of crime. Professor Cook suggested in a Sentencing Commission meeting that we might want to consider the use of jury awards for pain and suffering as a measure of the harm caused by crime. I am not sure how serious he was, but I took him up on using this idea. Thus credit (not blame) for some of my earliest work on the cost of crime must go to Phil Cook.

My first "cost of crime" estimates were published in 1988. Costs were now considerably higher and—at least in my mind—more realistic. For example, the "cost" of a rape was estimated to be $57,000—not $350! As a result, I recalculated the benefit–cost ratios set forth in Austin (1986) and came to the opposite conclusion. Letting prisoners out early in Illinois cost more in terms of the impact on crime victims than it saved taxpayer dollars by building fewer prisons. Thus, in my mind, to conclude that this early-release program was worthwhile was tantamount to balancing the state budget on the backs of crime victims.

The controversy surrounding my first article on the cost of crime did not take long to erupt. Anti-prison advocates quickly lambasted my methodology and targeted me as being a "right-wing" conservative. They correctly pointed out some of the methodological shortcomings in my earlier work, but also largely misunderstood the use and misuse of these data. Over time, my writings—which culminate in this book—address many of these concerns and explain how to interpret and appropriately use "cost-of-crime" data.

In 1998, I published a paper entitled "The Monetary Value of Saving a High Risk Youth." Once again, I must credit others with the basic idea behind this paper. Adele Harrell of the Urban Institute and Ed Zedlewski of the National Institute of Justice commissioned me to write this paper as part of an NIJ grant examining children at risk. At the time, Ed was pushing program-evaluators to conduct benefit–cost analyses. However, both Ed and Adele realized that they would be evaluating a program for children at risk many years before any crime-control benefits would accrue. Thus they asked me if I could answer a different question—if the program is to be deemed successful, how many children would have to be saved from a life of crime? From this question, "The Monetary Value of Saving a High Risk Youth" was born. This paper combined my "cost-of-crime" estimates with the number of crimes, years in prison, etc. for a high-risk youth who later becomes a career criminal. At the time, the paper concluded that a high-risk youth caused over $2 million in harm over his lifetime. The implication, of course, is that if one can design a program that "prevents" even one youth from going down this path—and it costs less than $2 million to prevent that one youth—the program pays for itself over time. This paper provided a rallying cry for non-profit organizations devoted to preventing crime through programs targeting at-risk youth. My findings are cited as proof that "prevention pays" all the time in funding proposals, websites on at-risk youth, etc. All of a sudden, I became a "left-wing" celebrity. Of course, I never said "prevention pays," but only that "prevention may pay." One still needs to determine whether the program works and at what cost.

Although I first published "cost-of-crime" estimates in 1988, it has taken quite a few years for policymakers to buy into the concept of benefit–cost analysis of criminal justice programs. However, over the past few years, there has been a dramatic surge of interest in this topic. I have been invited to give presentations to Justice Canada and the Home Office in the U.K.— both have commissioned studies on the cost of crime in their countries. In the U.K., the Home Office and the University of York established the new Centre for Criminal Justice Economics and Psychology, whose stated purpose includes a strong orientation toward the study of cost-effective crime control programs. A major study on the cost of crime was just completed in Australia. In March 2004 the European Union sponsored a conference in Helsinki where researchers and criminal justice officials from member states met to discuss and compare costs and benefits of crime prevention programs. This is the first international conference that I am aware of that focused on the costs of crime. The state of Washington has funded a serious research program to study the costs and benefits of crime control and prevention programs—the first such comprehensive program that directly feeds into policy decisions. Other states in the U.S. are following their lead. All of these signs are quite encouraging.

All along, I have attempted to keep personal views out of my objective, empirical analysis. This book reports on the state of the art in estimating crime costs. There are no political views expressed. The numbers might be used to show that some programs work and others do not. Let the chips fall where they may. All in the interest of more informed, better policy decisions . . .

# Acknowledgments

Over the years, I have benefited from many individuals who have worked as either co-authors, mentors, or assistants. As noted above, Phil Cook deserves the most thanks for inspiring me to work on this important topic and suggesting an early solution. He continues to be a mentor to me when I need him. Perhaps the person I have learned the most from over the years is Ted Miller, who is one of the world's leading experts on the cost of automobile crashes—for that matter, the cost of just about anything. I have teamed up with Ted on several occasions and have learned much from him. Special thanks must also go to current and former staff of the National Institute of Justice who have supported and encouraged much of my work in this area, especially Akiva Lieberman, Lois Mock, Richard Titus, Ed Zedlewski, and Betty Chemers. Jeff Roth, currently at the University of Pennsylvania's Jerry Lee Center of Criminology, deserves thanks for his leadership role in commissioning a paper on the cost of violence for the National Academy of Sciences Panel on Violence Research in the early 1990s.

Economists who delve into the criminology literature can often be looked upon with suspicion or simply ignored by mainstream criminologists. I have not found that to be the case. Instead, I have received nothing but encouragement, suggestions, citations, intellectually stimulating discussions, and critiques from some of the luminaries in the field, with special thanks to Al Blumstein, David Farrington, Daniel Nagin, and Larry Sherman. They have helped legitimize the use of "cost-of-crime" estimates and benefit–cost analysis in the criminal justice world.

Other co-authors and colleagues who deserve thanks include Roger Bowles, Adele Harrell, Colin Loftin, Cynthia McDougall, Roland Rust, Shelli Rossman, Sara Steen, Brian Wierseman, and Simon Tidd. Very capable research assistance has been provided by numerous students and researchers, including Gabrielle Chapman, Caterina Gouvis, Lisa Newmark, Achintya Ray, Naomi Limor Sedek, Mihir Shah, and Afsoun Yazdian. Special thanks to Robin, who over the years has been a wonderful proofreader as well as soulmate. Finally, to both Robin and Jenny, who have put up with my many long hours working at home on evenings and weekends . . . thanks for being so supportive.

# 1  Introduction and overview

On April 20, 1999, 17-year-old Dylan Kebold and 18-year-old Eric Harris walked into the Columbine High School in Littleton, Colorado and began a shooting rampage that was heard around the world. This single act of violence resulted in the death of 13 students and teachers, serious injuries to 28 others, and the death of the two gunmen. This tragedy certainly took its worst toll on the victims and their families. Although no amount of money can bring back the individuals whose lives were lost, the amount of money that was lost as a result of this incident was still enormous. There is no doubt that this incident caused the victims and their families to spend a significant amount of money on medical bills, caused them to lose time at work, and imposed other direct costs. Numerous indirect costs were also likely to have been incurred, such as the cost to families who took their children out of public schools and incurred private school tuition, or those who incurred the cost of moving to another school district or city. Charities around the world helped out, with an estimated $6 million being contributed directly to help families of victims (Washington, 1999). The fact that the murder victims will no longer earn a living means that over their expected future lifetime, hundreds of thousands and perhaps millions of dollars in earnings will have been lost. However, the loss to the victims and their families was considerably more than this amount. Any assessment of their loss must account for the tremendous pain, suffering, lost quality of life, and grief they suffered.

Many would argue that no amount of money would be adequate to compensate the victims or their families for this loss. We'll put that issue aside for now and return to it throughout this chapter and this book.

This act of violence affected others beside the families and victims. The impact and resultant costs were felt by thousands of friends, relatives, and neighbors who attended the funerals—perhaps taking time off work. They bought condolence cards and flowers, spent time visiting, brought food to the grieving family, and also suffered a non-trivial amount of grief and fear themselves. An estimated 70,000 people—many of whom traveled from out of town to express their grief—attended a memorial service for the community. Local florists donated 25,000 bouquets for the service as fighter jets flew overhead as a tribute (Serrano and Moehringer, 1999).

Schoolchildren who were not injured—but endured the five-hour ordeal—were traumatized and spent weeks or months with counselors and therapists. School was canceled for more than a week, and resumed half-days at a nearby high school. This tragedy was so massive that mental health providers were inundated for assistance. One report indicated that three weeks after the tragedy, "demand for care has not abated. One mental health provider in Littleton . . . said crisis calls have quadrupled and requests for ongoing services have gone up 50 percent. In the metro Denver area, managed care providers are reporting a 40 percent to 100 percent increase in requests for mental health services" (Cart, 1999). The mother of a victim who was left partially paralyzed committed suicide six months after the incident (Anonymous, 1999). For many, the consequences continue to this day.

The city government (and hence taxpayers) was also significantly affected by this act of violence. Police SWAT teams and investigators were needed to respond to this tragedy. Extra police were required to be on duty to help control traffic during the funeral and memorial services. The mayor's time was diverted from more productive activities to responding to reporters' questions and meeting with concerned citizens and the school board. Numerous lawsuits were filed by family members of victims against the city and police for not preventing and/or not adequately responding during the incident. While most of these lawsuits have since been dismissed, they were no doubt costly to the city of Littleton as well as the federal courts that processed them.

The indirect costs of the Columbine High School shooting went far beyond Colorado. Schools around the country reported high absenteeism rates in the days immediately following the incident, as students and parents feared copycat shootings (Samuels, 1999). Interest in home schooling increased dramatically as parents around the country developed a renewed interest in a safe alternative to public schools. In Colorado calls to the state Department of Education reportedly more than doubled following the shooting (Lloyd, 1999). Schools around the country reportedly have undergone expensive remodeling projects to enhance security in response to these shootings (Kass, 1999), have instituted training exercises for police, fire, and school officials, and hired additional security guards and police officers to patrol high schools (Wilgoren, 1999).

Although there has been no accounting of the total "cost" of the Columbine tragedy, it surely cost society hundreds of millions, if not billions, of dollars. Highly publicized cases such as this extreme case of school violence in the U.S. have highlighted the fact that although crime rates have been declining over the past decade, violence is still a significant social problem and the cost to society is no less real. Recent estimates have tallied the annual cost of crime to victims in the U.S. at about $450 billion. Attempts to incorporate other social costs into the equation suggest that the annual cost of crime to society is even larger—perhaps as much as $1 trillion or more. What do these numbers mean and what should they be used for?

How does crime compare to other social ills? This book provides a comprehensive review of the theoretical foundations, methodologies employed, and empirical estimates of the cost of crime. It also examines some of the possible uses—and misuses—of crime cost data.

A complete characterization of crime costs can be an important tool in formulating criminal justice policy. Identifying and quantifying costs and consequences of victimization may be helpful both in characterizing the crime problem and in examining ways to address it. Ignoring the non-monetary benefits of crime reduction can lead to a misallocation of resources. For will prevent one additional rape incident. Considering only tangible, out-of-pocket costs, the average rape (or attempted rape) costs $5,100—less than the $20–25,000 annual cost of a prison cell. The bulk of these expenses are medical and mental health care costs to victims. However, if rape's effect on the victim's quality of life is monetized along with other costs imposed on society at large, recent estimates indicate that society would be willing to pay about $237,000 to prevent one rape from occurring—many times greater than the cost of prison. Thus, from society's standpoint, it is worth spending $20,000 to $25,000 in additional prison costs in exchange for at least $237,000 in benefits from one less rape. Put differently, the "cost" to society of one rape is $237,000; hence it is certainly worth more than $25,000 to prevent one rape from occurring.

By allowing analysts to combine statistics on disparate crimes into a single, readily understood metric, monetary valuations of crime costs may be used to help guide resource allocations across crime types. For example, is a police patrol pattern that prevents a rape better than one that prevents three burglaries? One way to answer such a question is to ask residents of the affected area which they prefer through polling or referenda. However, in many instances, policymakers must rely on less direct methods of determining an appropriate choice. In such cases, one would need to have a metric that allows for comparisons between rapes and burglaries. Dollars provide such a metric for this comparison.

## Why do we need estimates of the "cost of crime?"

To most economists, there is no question that crime costs should be estimated. Economics involves the allocation of scarce resources in society. Criminal justice policy decisions always involve choices between two or more alternatives, each having their own costs and benefits. The enumeration of those costs and benefits puts the various alternatives on a level playing field and can help policymakers make more informed decisions that enhance society's well-being. Of course, if the enumerated costs and benefits are inaccurate, there is a risk that more information can lead to worse decisions. Further, many non-economists would argue that there is neither a moral justification nor adequate empirical basis for placing dollar values on intangible factors such as pain, suffering, and lost quality of life. I will return to these issues later in this chapter. For now, please indulge this economist and "assume" that such intangibles can be measured. I want to highlight three important policy-relevant purposes of measuring costs and benefits:

- comparison of the relative harm caused by type of crime,
- comparison of the aggregate harm from crime with other social ills, and
- benefit–cost analysis of alternative crime control policies.

Martin and Bradley (1964) provide a more detailed discussion of the importance of identifying and quantifying the costs of crime.

### Relative harm by type of crime

Policymakers are often interested in comparing the harm caused by different types of crime. For example, most advocates of sentencing guidelines rely on victim harm as one component of their sentencing structure. Those who subscribe to a "just deserts" philosophy of punishment combine harm with culpability, whereas those who advocate a utilitarian approach combine harm with detectability and deterrability. Although one can tally up the various harms associated with each type of crime (e.g. value of property stolen, frequency of injuries by type of injury, mental health related injuries), without a common metric such as dollars, it is difficult to objectively compare these harms.

A few non-monetary metrics have been proposed for comparing harms— such as number of days for a victim to recoup the financial loss or the number of life years lost (see e.g. Maltz, 1975). These are primarily designed to overcome the perceived unfairness of valuing harms according to the wealth of the individual being harmed.[1] However, these proposals also suffer from not having a common metric. One is still unable to compare 100 lost workdays to one lost life year, for example.

Absent a common metric to compare harms, the generally accepted approach to rank the severity of crimes has been to survey the public (see Wolfgang *et al.*, 1985; Cullen, Link, and Polanzi, 1982; Rossi *et al.*, 1974). These surveys ask respondents to rank the seriousness of various crimes, and result in relatively consistent rankings over time and across populations. An alternative method is to ask respondents what actual prison sentences they believe should be meted out for different crime scenarios (see Rossi and Berk, 1997). However, these studies are based on subjective public perceptions concerning the severity of crimes—which may include misperceptions about the frequency of injuries in typical criminal events. For example, Cohen (1988a) argues that public-perception surveys tend to underestimate the harm associated with violent crimes relative to property crimes. These studies are also generally unable to distinguish between the generic harm associated with an injury and the actual consequences of any particular victimization. This would be particularly important if one were interested in the extent to which the consequences of victimization vary across communities or different segments of the population (e.g. age or sex), for example. Despite these limitations, public-perception surveys have recently been used in a slightly different context—by eliciting the public's willingness to pay for reduced crime. As we will discuss later in this chapter, assessing the public's willingness to pay is conceptually a better approach than many other methods that have been used to measure the monetary value of crime.

## Aggregate costs and benefits

One of the most common—yet probably least important—reasons for estimating the costs of crime is to tally up the aggregate cost to society. Multibillion-dollar cost estimates can easily make their way into the popular press and political debate. There are two basic problems with tallying up the costs of crime. First, having been told that crime costs the U.S. $450 billion per year, what are we to do with this information? If we are successful in fully estimating the aggregate cost of crime, we can compare this total cost estimate to that of other social problems (e.g. cancer, auto crashes, homelessness). Whether one agrees that this is a useful exercise or not, various advocacy groups do compare "cost-of-crime" estimates to the cost of other social ills in an effort to affect policy decisions. Unfortunately, misuses of these data occur on both sides of the political debate.

Until recently, most estimates of the cost of crime (including estimates published by the Bureau of Justice Statistics) have significantly underestimated costs. For example, Irwin and Austin (1994) used the "official" government estimates of $19 billion to illustrate that crime is less of a problem than other social ills and to argue against increased prison sentences. A more comprehensive cost study sponsored by the National Institute of Justice reports the annual cost of crime to victims to be $450 billion (Miller, Cohen, and Wiersema, 1996). An article reporting on that study in the *New York Times* quoted a Republican Congressman as saying the report "demonstrates that the cost of building prisons and adding police are justified" (Butterfield, 1996). Despite the rhetoric, neither small nor large "cost-of-crime" numbers demonstrate that the cost of building more prisons is justified or that alternatives to incarceration are better than more prisons!

Even if properly measured,[2] one cannot simply compare aggregate cost estimates of crime with estimates of the cost of other social ills to arrive at policy recommendations for future public spending priorities. Suppose, for example, that the cost of crime in the U.S. was estimated to exceed the cost of auto crashes. This does not necessarily mean that society should increase expenditures on crime prevention relative to prevention of auto crashes. If the costs of "preventing" crimes and auto crashes are factored into the equation, it might be found that society is already spending too much on the former and not enough on the latter. The more relevant question is how much additional reduction in crimes (or auto crashes) we would observe if we spent more on prevention. This can only be answered if we know such things as the deterrent and incapacitative effect of various sanctions, increased police patrols, etc.

Subject to the above caveat, comparing cost estimates of crime with other social ills can provide a basis of comparison on a common metric. For example, a study by Streff *et al.* (1992) estimated that the total cost of traffic crashes in Michigan was about three times as much as the total cost of crime in that state. Although no immediate policy implications should be drawn from this comparison, it does help begin the process of identifying public policy priorities and puts crime into its proper perspective. Over time, it might also be possible to quantify the magnitude of any change in crime rates by comparing costs from year to year.

A second problem with tallying up the costs of crime is that the true cost of crime is more than the sum total of its parts. If there were no robbers or rapists in this world, hitchhiking would probably be a way of life for a huge portion of the population. If violence was totally eliminated from society, organized crime might evaporate (as it depends on the threat of violence for its survival), and the standard of living of many inner city residents would increase as businesses returned to previously abandoned storefronts. These massive changes in social structure could only come about with equally impressive changes in social behavior. Thus any truly aggregate estimates of the cost of crime would need to account for these factors. To date, most estimates of the cost of crime have been done incrementally—for example, what is the cost of one crime given the current level of crime, or what is the value of reducing crime by 10 percent.

### Benefit–cost analysis of crime control policies

Perhaps the most important—and controversial—use of monetary estimates of the cost of crime is to compare the benefits and costs of alternative crime control policies.[3] There is no shortage of crime prevention and crime reduction programs and proposals that would benefit from government funding. However, the government can only fund so many of these programs. One of the benefits of using dollars as a common metric for analyzing criminal justice policy is that society spends dollars to try to prevent crime from occurring in the first place. Society's ability to control criminal behavior and reduce the incidence of victimization is limited by its ability to pay for police, courts, corrections, and prevention programs. In an effort to reduce crime and the severity of its consequences, society has undertaken many criminal justice experiments, including intensive probation, electronic monitoring of offenders, shock incarceration, targeted and community police, spouse arrest programs for domestic violence, etc. As new policies are tested and policy options are considered, one must be able to apply objective evaluation techniques.[4] If two options have identical crime control effects but differing costs, the choice is simple. Unfortunately, few policy alternatives are so easily compared. In a more realistic case where a new policy reduces crime at some additional expense (or crime increases with less expenditures), one of the key questions is whether that reduced (increased) crime is worth its cost. Only by monetizing the cost of crime can one begin to answer that question.

One of the most compelling reasons to monetize the costs and benefits of crime control programs—and to attempt a benefit–cost analysis—is the consequence of not doing so. Whenever a criminal justice or prevention program is adopted or not adopted, society is implicitly conducting a benefit–cost analysis and placing dollar values on crimes. For example, suppose one program costs $1 million and ultimately will prevent 100 burglaries from occurring. Whether made explicit or not, the policymaker adopting that program has determined that it is worth spending at least $10,000 to reduce each burglary ($1 million divided by 100 burglaries). If another $1 million program that was not funded would have prevented 50 serious physical assaults from occurring, the policymaker is implicitly determining that each assault is worth less than $20,000 ($1 million divided by 50). Thus even the policymaker who has ethical concerns about placing dollar values on crime and conducting benefit–cost analysis implicitly makes a value judgment about the monetary value of crime.

## History of cost-of-crime estimates

The idea of measuring the monetary costs of crime and the monetary benefits of crime reduction has been around for many years. Estimates of the cost of crime have a long history, dating back as early as the 1931 Wickersham Commission. A review of some of these studies is contained in Gray (1979). Subsequent presidential commissions have been called upon to report on the cost of crime. Many of these reports noted the difficulty and lack of progress over the years in adequately capturing the full costs of crime. However, they also acknowledged the importance of continuing this line of research. These earlier studies tended to report broad aggregates and focus on direct costs such as victim's out-of-pocket costs, the criminal justice system, the cost of private security, and the value of illegal wagers.

The National Crime Victim Survey (NCVS), sponsored by the U.S. Bureau of Justice Statistics, is an annual survey of U.S. households that gathers data on the rate of victimization in the U.S. Among the questions asked of victims identified by the survey, are several questions that directly relate to the cost of crime and violence. Victims are asked about medical expenses, lost workdays and property stolen or damaged. From these questions, national estimates of the out-of-pocket costs per criminal offense can be made (Klaus, 1994). Although used by some researchers in the past, the NCVS estimates of the "economic cost of crime" are now widely regarded as inadequate. As discussed further in Chapter 2, the NCVS estimates are known to significantly underestimate even the out-of-pocket costs of crime and do not even begin to examine indirect and intangible costs.

The earlier studies—and the official government surveys—did not go beyond the out-of-pocket "tangible costs" of victimization. Beginning with Thaler (1978), there have been several attempts to include intangible costs. Thaler examined the price of housing in Rochester, N.Y. and inferred home-owners' willingness to pay for reduced crime by estimating property value differences in high- versus low-crime areas. In theory, homeowners are willing to pay to avoid the risk of both the tangible costs and intangible costs of being a crime victim. Various studies have since replicated and improved on these results for different cities and different time spans, with broadly consistent results. A major limitation in these hedonic property value studies of crime is that they have only estimated the cost of a generic index crime (rape, robbery, assault, motor vehicle theft, burglary and larceny combined). Owing to data limitations, previous studies have been unable to disentangle the cost of individual crimes. Bartley (2000) was only somewhat successful in isolating the cost of individual crimes using a much larger data set than previously.

Phillips and Votey (1981) took a different approach by combining esti-mates of the value of a statistical life with crime seriousness rankings from public surveys. Their approach was the first to attempt to account for the intangible costs of individual crimes, but it still was not able to account for many of those intangible costs. Cohen (1988a, 1988b) and subsequent follow-up studies by Cohen, Miller, and Rossman (1994) and Miller, Cohen, and Wiersema (1996) have taken a different approach to estimating the cost of crime. That approach combines estimates of the direct out-of-pocket costs with intangible losses estimated from a combination of jury awards in per-sonal injury lawsuits and the value of a statistical life. This approach permits researchers to apply cost estimates to individual crime types. However, it is not entirely a market-based approach. Pain and suffering for non-fatal injuries are based on subjective jury awards in similar cases.[5] Although a good argument can be made that the jury award system is a reasonable mech-anism to derive social costs, economists would generally prefer to impute dollar values from actual market transactions. That is why the property value approach was so appealing and is still mentioned by most economists as the preferred method of estimating the cost of crime. In Chapter 2 we will examine this methodology and its criticisms in detail. More recently, however, economists have begun to employ a new method, called "contin-gent valuation," which is also discussed in more detail in Chapter 2.

## The scope of this book and crime costs

As we saw with the Columbine High School example, one criminal event can impose numerous types of cost on many different parties. Victims and their families suffer in many ways—medical costs, earnings losses, property damage, lost quality of life, etc. Sometimes those costs are borne by the victims and their families, oftentimes society pays for these costs through insurance premiums or higher taxes.

The economics-of-crime literature has traditionally distinguished between three types of cost (Demmert, 1979: 2–5):

- those caused directly by criminal behavior (i.e. external costs imposed by the offender),
- those costs society incurs in response to crime to deter or prevent future incidents or to exact retribution, and
- those costs incurred by the offender (such as the opportunity cost of the offender's time while either engaging in the offense or being punished, if he or she otherwise could have been employed in productive activity).

Not all of these costs have been quantified. However, it is useful to enumerate all categories of crime, which is done below.

### Costs imposed directly as a result of crime

Table 1.1 (overleaf) summarizes the various costs of crime. Victims incur many direct out-of-pocket expenses such as stolen or damaged property, medical costs, lost wages while away from work, and mental health or other victim-related treatment. Even if medical costs are reimbursed through insurance or employee benefit programs, society bears the cost through higher insurance premiums. Since the provision of insurance requires administrative (overhead) costs, the loss is even higher than the medical cost itself. If the employee receives paid sick leave or workers compensation during the recovery period, the employer bears the cost of the paid wages and the administrative cost of processing the payments. The employer may even have higher expenses owing to lost productivity or the need to hire temporary help or to pay overtime in the interim. Thus the total "out-of-pocket" portion of injury costs is actually higher than the sum of property losses, medical costs, and lost wages.

Although some costs are incurred as a direct result of victimization, other costs are more indirect—yet no less real. For example, victims might take new precautions such as avoiding certain areas of town, incurring longer commute times and/or more expensive means of transportation. These actions are often called "avoidance behavior." Some victims who now feel unsafe in their neighborhoods may incur the expense associated with moving (selling and buying a house, higher rent, moving expenses, etc.). Others might buy new protection devices such as burglar alarms, guard dogs, or defensive weapons.

Another indirect cost often associated with injuries is a temporary or permanent inability to do housework. In some cases, the family of the victim

*Table 1.1* The costs of crime—a typology

| Cost category | Party who most directly bears cost |
| --- | --- |
| **I COSTS OF CRIME** | |
| Productivity losses | |
| 1 Lost workdays | |
| (a) Lost wages for unpaid workdays | Victim |
| (b) Lost productivity | Society/employer |
| (c) Temporary labor and training of replacements | Society/employer |
| 2 Lost housework | Victim and family |
| 3 Lost school days | |
| (a) Forgone wages owing to lack of education | Victim |
| (b) Forgone non-pecuniary benefits of education | Victim |
| (c) Forgone social benefits owing to lack of education | Society |
| Medical and mental health care | |
| 1 Costs not reimbursed by victim family | Victim/victim's family/society |
| 2 Costs reimbursed by insurance | Society |
| 3 Administrative cost: insurance reimbursement | Society |
| Direct property losses | |
| 1 Losses not reimbursed by insurance | Victim |
| 2 Losses reimbursed by insurance . | Society |
| 3 Administrative cost: insurance reimbursement | Society |
| 4 Administrative cost: recovery and processing by police | Society |
| Indirect costs of victimization | |
| 1 Avoidance behavior | Victim |
| 2 Expenditures on moving, alarms, guard dogs, etc. | Victim |
| Pain and suffering/quality of life | Victim |
| Loss of affection/enjoyment | Victim's family |
| Death | |
| 1 Lost quality of life | Victim |
| 2 Loss of affection/enjoyment | Victim's family |
| 3 Funeral and burial expenses | Victim's family |
| 4 Psychological injury/treatment | Victim's family |
| Legal costs associated with tort claims | Victim/victim's family/third party |
| Victim services | |
| 1 Expenses charged to victim | Victim |
| 2 Expenses paid by agency | Society |
| "Second-generation costs" | |
| 1 Future victims of crime committed by earlier victims | Future victim |
| 2 Future social costs associated with (1) | Society, etc. |
| **II COST OF SOCIETY'S RESPONSE TO CRIME** | |
| Avoidance costs | |
| 1 Avoidance behavior | Potential victim |
| 2 Expenditures on moving, alarms, guard dogs, etc. | Potential victim |

| Cost category | Party who most directly bears cost |
|---|---|
| Fear of crime | Potential victim |
| Criminal justice system | Society |
| 1 Police and investigative costs | Society |
| 2 Prosecutors | Society |
| 3 Courts | Society |
| 4 Legal fees | |
| (a) public defenders | Society |
| (b) private legal fees | Offenders |
| 5 Incarceration costs | Society |
| 6 Non-incarcerative sanctions | Society |
| 7 Victim/family time | Victim/family |
| 8 Jury and witness time | Jury/witness |
| Victim services | |
| 1 Victim service organizations | Society |
| 2 Victim service volunteer time | Volunteers |
| 3 Victim compensation programs | Society/offender |
| 4 Victim/family time | Victim/family |
| Other non-criminal justice programs | |
| 1 Hot-lines and public service announcements | Society |
| 2 Community treatment programs | Society |
| 3 Private therapy/counseling | Society/offender |
| Incarcerated offender costs | |
| 1 Lost wages | Offender/family |
| 2 Lost tax revenue and productivity | Society |
| 3 Value of lost freedom | Offender |
| 4 Psychological cost to family/loss of consortium | Family of offender |
| "Overdeterrence" costs | |
| 1 Innocent individuals accused of offense | Innocent individuals |
| 2 Restriction of legitimate activity | Innocent individuals |
| 3 Actions taken by offenders to avoid detection e.g. kill robbery victims to reduce chance of being caught | Society/offender victim |
| "Justice" costs | |
| 1 Constitutional protections to avoid false accusations | Society |
| 2 Cost of increasing detection rate to avoid differential punishment | Society |

## III OFFENDER COSTS

| | |
|---|---|
| Opportunity cost of time spent in illegal activity instead of "working" | Society |
| Resources devoted to illegal activity (e.g. guns) | Offender |

Source: Adapted and expanded from Cohen, Miller, and Rossman (1994), Tables 1 and 2.

might hire someone to replace all or part of those household services, such as a maid, lawn care service or babysitter. The cost of hiring replacement services is clearly a monetary loss experienced by the family. In other cases, however, family members devote additional time to make up for the inability of the victim to carry out some of these chores. Although little or no monetary loss might be associated with this form of lost housework, one can estimate the monetary value of the replaced housework using economic principles and market wage rates.

Lost schoolwork for a student might also be valued. In the worst cases, a significant amount of school is missed and a victim might be set back a year in school. In other cases, the loss in education might be temporary and be made up through additional hours of work outside the classroom or result in lowered performance on exams. Although valuing these lost school days is difficult, in theory victims lose potential future earnings and the "psychic" value of an education. The potential cost of missed school days goes beyond the victim, as society values an educated population beyond the amount that the average individual would be willing to invest by him/herself.

In addition to the tangible costs incurred by victims (or paid by third parties), many other "intangible" consequences of crime may be quantified in monetary terms. One of the potentially largest intangible costs associated with victim injury is pain and suffering. Although pain and suffering do not involve a monetary loss, they may be monetized for purposes of comparison with other costs. Related to pain and suffering is the potential cost associated with the inability to continue some enjoyable leisure activities. These might be called "quality-of-life" costs. Not surprisingly, these costs are much more difficult to estimate than tangible costs, a subject that we will examine in some detail in chapter 2.

In addition to the victim, the victim's family may incur costs. One cost mentioned earlier is any additional expense incurred or time spent by family members doing chores previously performed by the family member who was injured and is no longer able to do these household chores. Another cost labeled "loss of affection/enjoyment" involves spousal and family activities that the victim can no longer participate in due to the injury.

Costs also arise when injured victims die. In addition to such costs as lost future wages and premature funeral and burial expenses, the value of the life itself is lost. Unlike other victim losses, the victim cannot be compensated for his/her life. However, various techniques are available to place monetary values on the statistical value of life.

In some cases, victims of violent behavior (or their families) may bring a private tort action against the party who injured the victim (or a third party for negligence). These suits involve various legal and court costs—often to third parties and insurance companies.

Finally, we should consider the long-term consequences of violent crime. For example, there is some evidence that victims of child abuse are more likely to become child abusers themselves. To the extent that the causal connection can be made, one should consider the future cost associated with child abuse to be a cost of today's incident.

### Cost of society's response to crime

In addition to the cost imposed by the offender onto the victim, society's response to victimization involves many different types of cost. These costs are summarized in the second part of Table 1.1. Crime also has an impact on people who are not directly victimized, by increasing the level of fear in potential victims. Although difficult in practice, one can envision placing a dollar value on the level of fear in potential victims. Further, fear of victimization might result in increased prevention expenditures on items such as security systems and defensive firearms. It might also lead to changes in behavior, such as taking fewer walks at night.

The most visible cost associated with preventing future victimization is the criminal justice system. This includes government expenditures for police, prosecutors, public defenders, courts, prisons, and other non-incarcerative sanctions. It also includes private expenditures on criminal defense lawyers, as well as the amount of time spent by victims, juries, and witnesses dealing with the criminal justice system.

Some of society's response to violent behavior falls outside the criminal justice arena, with programs such as community treatment facilities and public service announcements, and prevention programs targeted at high-risk youth. Whether or not they are effective in preventing injuries or in raising the awareness of others to the problem, society spends resources attempting to publicize the problem and to prevent further incidents such as child physical and sexual abuse, drug abuse, juvenile delinquency, and long-term criminal careers.

Not only does violent behavior impose costs on the victim but some costs fall directly on the offender who is apprehended and subject to the criminal justice system. Other costs are borne by the offender's family. For example, if the offender was working prior to incarceration, he/she will suffer from lost wages while in prison. Regardless of whether or not one wants to include the offender's well-being as part of society's interests, those lost wages are a measure of the productivity loss to society. There is also evidence that incarceration will reduce the future earning capacity of many offenders as they have a more difficult time finding quality employment with a felony record. Potentially more costly is the intangible loss to the family—especially children—of the incarcerated offender.

A second potential cost is the value of lost freedom to an incarcerated offender. Beyond the social productivity loss, some would argue that society should consider the impact that prison has on the offender. A related and potentially more troubling cost associated with incarceration of offenders is the risk that the prison experience will increase the propensity of the offender to recidivate. To the extent that this is true, if one were to compare the cost of imprisonment to the cost of probation (for example), any marginal increase in future crimes should be attributed to the cost of imprisonment.

Finally, two often-overlooked categories of cost are "overdeterrence" and "justice" costs. Although these costs are likely to be relatively small in terms of the overall cost of victimization, it is important to enumerate them, since they have significant policy implications.

Overdeterrence costs are collateral consequences of imposing penalties for violent behavior. First, innocent parties who might be accused of committing a crime will take costly actions to avoid such allegations. Second, violent offenders might increase their level of violence in order to reduce the risk of capture.

The cost of "justice" is primarily determined by society's willingness to take costly precautions to ensure innocent individuals are not accused of crimes. Additional "justice" costs are incurred to the extent that society chooses more costly crime control alternatives than would be required if the concern was solely with minimizing the cost for a given level of deterrence.

### Offender costs

Finally, the last section of Table 1.1 enumerates offender costs. Note that costs imposed upon offenders by a society that wishes to punish, rehabilitate, or otherwise seek justice were included above under the category "society's response to violence." Here we consider costs that are incurred by the offender or society directly as a result of being involved in criminal activity. For example, offenders might spend considerable time and/or resources committing the violent act. Although all of these costs are borne by the offender directly, society would also benefit from their absence. The most obvious cost would be the opportunity cost of the offender's time. That is, if the offender could have been gainfully employed while not engaging in criminal behavior, society is losing that productivity. In addition, one might consider other resource costs that assist the offender in carrying out this behavior—such as expenditures on weapons.

## Remainder of the book

In the next chapter, we will examine the theoretical framework and empirical methodologies used to estimate the cost of crime. This involves the use of economic concepts and statistical methodologies. Although sometimes these concepts and techniques are quite technical, I assume the reader has only a minimal economics and statistics background. The techniques employed by economists who place dollar values on crime is not without controversy. Thus the next chapter also considers the criticisms of that approach. The remainder of the book examines various components of the cost of crime in more detail and provides actual dollar estimates where available. Chapter 3 examines the cost to victims. Chapter 4 considers the cost to third parties and to society in general, while Chapter 5 looks at the use of cost-of-crime estimates in policy analysis of criminal justice and crime prevention programs.

# 2 An economic approach to crime and costing methodologies

Understanding the cost-of-crime literature requires some basic familiarity with several important economic concepts. This chapter provides a non-technical review of the fundamental economic principles underlying the cost-of-crime literature. The purpose of providing this background is to give the reader enough knowledge to understand the proper uses and limitations of these estimates. Different methodologies for estimating costs will also be considered. Some of these alternative methodologies have only been employed in a limited fashion. Finally, recent attempts to estimate the costs of crime have been criticized by some authors. These critiques are reviewed in some detail.

The methods one uses to estimate the cost of crime are very much dependent on how one defines costs. In this book, I take an economic approach to defining costs. This section explains the underlying theory behind estimating costs and distinguishes between various types of cost. We first begin with the economic theory of crime.

## Economic theory of crime

Economics is the study of the allocation of scarce resources. For each good or service that is traded in the marketplace, there is a "supply" and "demand" that ultimately determine its price and quantity sold. Some goods and services are not formally traded through normal marketplaces. Examples of such "non-market" goods (or "bads") are pollution, government services, and crime. It is often useful to consider the "supply" and "demand" of such non-market goods and services. This paradigm is especially useful in thinking about violence (Cook, 1986). Although people do not normally buy and sell the right to be victimized (or to be free of victimization), markets do exist that affect the likelihood of being victimized. That offenders "supply" violence is perhaps most obvious. But do they respond to economic incentives in a manner similar to supply curves in economics? In economics, if the price in the marketplace is increased or the cost of producing the good decreases, more firms will supply the good in question. Similarly, if the "expected cost" of committing an offense (e.g. the risk of going to jail and/or the expected severity of punishment) increases, we expect there to be fewer offenses.

The economic theory of crime generally postulates that a potential offender will weigh the expected cost of committing the crime (probability of being caught multiplied by the sanction if caught) against the expected benefit (value of stolen property or "utility" the criminal receives from offending behavior). Even if some potential offenders are intent on committing the crime, they might take costly actions to reduce their chance of being punished. Thus they might use an accomplice to watch for police, buy more sophisticated equipment to break into cars more quickly, etc. On the other hand, some potential offenders will find that the expected reward from crime is now less than the expected cost. Similarly, if the "opportunity cost" of devoting time to criminal activity increases, potential offenders are likely to reduce their criminal activity. Thus we expect the supply of crime to decrease when good jobs in the legitimate sector are plentiful, and to increase when unemployment is high. In fact, several studies have confirmed this theory, by showing that crime rises and falls with the business cycle and the ups and downs of the economy (see Cook and Zarkin, 1985; and Freeman, 1996).

What about the "demand" side of the market? Potential victims can take costly actions such as installing burglar alarms, taking cabs instead of walking in high-crime areas, purchasing defensive firearms, and taking lessons in self-defense. All of these activities might affect the potential victim's chances of being victimized. Although potential victims do not actually "demand" crime, they do demand—and devote considerable resources to trying to achieve—reductions in their chances of being victimized. Thus they "demand" less crime. Similarly, by not taking certain preventive measures, one might argue that the action of potential offenders is similar to a "demand" for more crime.

Although private individuals become the victims of crime, a large part of the "market" for crime is handled through the public sector. The public sector takes on a lot of these responsibilities because crime reduction has many attributes of a "public" good. Examples of other public goods are national defense and pollution control. A public good is one in which people who "consume" the good cannot exclude others from consuming. Thus although it might be in everyone's best interest to contribute to a private effort to reduce pollution or to decrease the supply of crime, since those who do not contribute still enjoy the benefits of these efforts, many people will 'free ride' off the expenditures of others. Thus the private marketplace would not supply enough of that good if left to market forces, and the government might be able to make all citizens better off by taxing them and providing the services directly. Drug treatment programs, law enforcement, and corrections are all ways in which society attempts to affect the "supply" of crime.

Although by its very definition, crime is "bad" and socially harmful, so

### Are violent criminals rational?

The economic model of the demand and supply of crime is largely based on an assumption of rational actors. However, many violent crimes are crimes of passion, where rationality might be questioned. Does this mean that the economic model of crime is flawed? Not necessarily. First, many violent crimes occur in the commission of property offenses (e.g. robbery or burglary where someone is home) or in drug transactions. These are not crimes of passion, but are often calculated offenses carried out by rational individuals. Second, even if perpetrators are not entirely rational—and do not respond to expected sanctions—we can raise the cost of their committing the offense in the first place. For example, we can make it difficult for convicted felons to obtain firearms, issue restraining orders against stalkers, and even incarcerate or institutional-ize serious offenders who are likely to continue their violent behaviors. We can also reduce the opportunities for people to commit crime by increasing lighting in parking lots or installing extra locks—thus increas-ing the cost of committing a crime. Third, even for crimes of passion, we must recall that there is both a supply and a demand side of the equa-tion. Potential victims can take costly actions to reduce their risk of becoming victimized—i.e. reduce their "demand" for violence.

Empirical research has demonstrated that crime rates can be affected by the deterrent effect of longer prison sentences. For example, a study by economist Steven Levitt (1996) estimated that for each 10 percent increase in a state's prison population, robberies fall 7 percent, assault and burglary drop by 4 percent each, auto theft and larceny decline 3 percent each, rape falls 2.5 percent and murder drops 1.5 percent. Thus the economic paradigm is a useful way to examine crime and justice policies.

This does not mean that economics is the only tool required. Cer-tainly, social values of fairness, justice, and concern over convicting the innocent are valid goals. Economics does not tell us what we should value—i.e. it does not tell us whether or not we should value "fairness." However, even here, economics can help inform the debate by explicitly identifying the trade-offs involved in our value judg-ments. Thus it is useful to know, for example, that society spends millions of dollars on a capital punishment trial as opposed to the much lower amount that is spent on a murder trial where the death penalty is not being sought. This allows for a more informed decision and explicitly identifies the "cost" of our decision to allow capital punishment. (Of course, one would also want to make explicit any differences in the deterrent effect of capital punishment or other costs and benefits of each alternative.)

are the resources devoted to catching criminals, punishing them, and avoiding them. Thus the economic approach to crime control is concerned with finding the optimal combination of prevention, detection, enforcement, and offending behavior. Put differently, although we would all like there to be zero crime, we must recognize the fact that this is an unattainable goal— primarily because of the costs involved in preventing, detecting, and punishing criminal activity. Thus, in economics, we talk about there being an "optimal" level of crime.

The concept of an "optimal" level of crime may appear to be morally repugnant to people who believe the government should attempt to eradicate all social evils. In particular, it might be difficult to accept the fact that there will always be some crime and that public policymakers will in effect "permit" some crime to exist. Yet both private citizens and policymakers make such difficult decisions every day.

Consider the petty crime of purse snatching. There are many decision-makers involved in the "supply and demand" for purse snatching. By employing elaborate preventive security measures or very severe penalties we might reduce the level of this crime, or if security is sufficiently onerous, perhaps eliminate it completely. Women who carry purses might decide to alter the type of purse to buy—a consideration that might include not just fashion, but also the design of the purse in making it less of a target for theft. Potential victims might take other precautions such as possessing extra credit cards that are kept at home, carrying less cash than they might otherwise keep on hand (requiring them to make more trips to the bank), avoiding certain neighborhoods or shopping districts which purse snatchers are more likely to frequent, etc. Implicitly, in deciding what actions to take, potential victims will weigh the costs of these precautionary actions against the expected benefits of reducing the probability that they will become victimized.

Potential victims are not the only actors in this little drama. Store owners in neighborhoods where purse snatchers are known to be numerous might believe that potential customers are staying away and that they would personally benefit from reducing crime on their streets. They might install extra lighting or security cameras, again weighing the cost of those prevention activities against the additional profits they expect to receive from increased business. However, if the costs of the extra security exceed their anticipated profits, they are unlikely to provide this protection. Ultimately, the store-owner selects a level of security, and hence implicitly a positive level of crime, that she believes will result in maximum net profits.

Local government authorities might also take similar precautions or add more police on the street. Purse snatching is a crime, and one that results in punishment for the offender who is convicted. When potential victims and storeowners decide how much to spend on protective activities and potential purse snatchers decide whether to engage in illegal activity, knowledge about what the criminal justice system will likely do in response to purse snatching will be important to all of these actors. What is the likelihood that the purse snatcher will be caught? If caught, how much time must the victim spend away from work or the home in order to deal with the criminal justice system? How expensive is it for the government to prosecute and convict the purse snatcher? What sanction will the judge impose for this offense? All of these questions are important and interrelated. For example, if judges are reluctant to impose any significant sanction on purse snatchers, prosecutors might decline the cases or accept minimal plea bargains or pretrial diversions. But that does not necessarily mean purse snatching will increase dramatically. If the risk of being penalized by the criminal justice system decreases, potential victims and storeowners may increase their surveillance and preventive measures, as these forms of preventive expenditures become more cost-effective relative to punishment. However, if the sanction is very severe—so that purse snatchers are guaranteed significant prison time, for example, storeowners and potential victims will shift some of the cost of prevention onto the criminal justice system. Thus fewer storeowners will purchase costly security systems and lighting that help reduce crime, and instead they will rely on the deterrent effect of strict sentencing to reduce purse snatching. Potential victims might also take fewer precautions knowing that the risk of purse snatching is lower owing to the government's increased penalties.

So far, we have talked mostly about potential victims and the government. But, of course, one of the most important decisionmakers in this story is the potential purse snatcher himself. Certainly, the risk of being caught and punished will enter into his decision about whether to commit the crime. But so will other factors—such as the opportunities for legitimate employment as an alternative to illegal means of obtaining money. Another factor might simply be the extent to which social pressures and norms "punish" purse snatchers and hurt the reputation of those convicted of this crime. Does being a convicted felon reduce someone's ability to find employment? Does it reduce their reputation in the community or within their family?

As you can see from this little example, how much purse snatching there is in a community depends on the decisions of numerous actors—including potential victims, offenders, and the government. Each of these actors implicitly weighs the costs and benefits they receive from this crime in determining their optimal response. To the extent that costs are eliminated, society benefits and the public is safer. More importantly for policy analysis, one needs to keep in mind the fact that these costs are interdependent.

Figure 2.1 illustrates these theoretical links between the various cost components. Starting at the upper left-hand corner, the government might spend money to prevent crime. Suppose, for example, that additional police are hired and put on the street. In isolation, this is a bad thing since it increases the external costs associated with crime. Of course, the reason additional police are likely to have been hired in the first place is the expectation that it will lead to a reduction in crime. If indeed this happens, it will presumably result in a net cost decrease—if the additional cost of hiring police is less

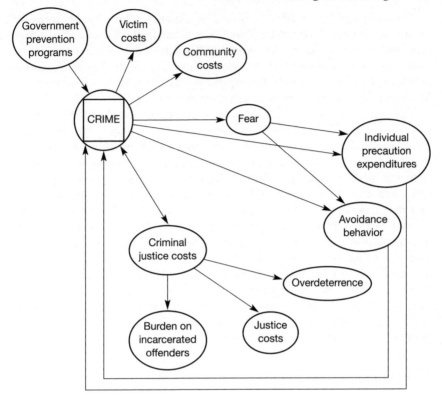

*Figure 2.1* The costs of crime

than the costs that would have been imposed by the crimes that were averted. Reduced crime results in reduced victim costs. It might also reduce fear of crime and enhance the nearby community business activity. Fear of crime leads to individuals taking costly avoidance behaviors such as buying burglar alarms or taking taxis instead of walking at night. If people feel safer, they might reduce these precautionary expenditures and avoidance behaviors. Note, however, that Figure 2.1 also contains a feedback loop from avoidance and precautionary expenditures into crime. If the supply of crime goes down because we incarcerate more criminals, potential victims might feel safer and be more apt to walk in the park at night. However, the fact that there are now more vulnerable victims in the park at night might induce new offenders into the crime market.

In addition to having an effect on victims and communities, changes in the crime rate result in changes in criminal justice costs. In this case, the lower crime rate brought about by spending dollars on police will not only reduce the cost to the government of running the criminal justice system, it might also reduce some of the costs imposed through incarcerated offenders.

Thus, ultimately, in addition to simply tallying up the costs of crime, we want to understand the linkages that exist between these cost components. Although we can specify the theoretical linkages that we expect to find based on both economic and behavioral theories, one of the challenges for criminal justice researchers is to empirically determine how important these linkages really are and how they affect crime rates.

The discussion thus far has focused on the supply and demand for crime. But this is a book about the "cost" of crime. The reason I introduced this chapter with the notion of a market for crime is that one of the key ingredients needed to determine how much time and money should be devoted to reducing either the supply or demand for crime is the cost imposed by crime. If the worst violent crimes in the U.S. consisted of a "slap on the wrist," the fact that this results in little "cost" to the victim would prompt potential victims and government policymakers to shift their resources out of reducing crime and into other more costly problems such as pollution, food safety, or other social issues. Similarly, if violent crime became more violent as illegal firearms became more prevalent or offenders became inherently more aggressive, the "cost" of crime would become higher and the "value" of trying to reduce the supply and demand of crime would increase. Thus good criminal justice policy requires that we understand the cost of crime in order to target our resources effectively.

## Definition of "costs"

A rose is a rose by any other name, but not all costs are the same and they cannot be treated equally. Some costs are incurred by only one individual, while others are borne by society as a whole. Some costs are tangible—money is actually paid or lost—while others are intangible and no money transfer actually takes place. The latter are much more difficult to measure and more controversial. Some costs are estimated based on "averages" while others are based on "marginal" analysis. Some costs are directly imposed by the offender (e.g. medical costs), while others are only indirectly imposed (such as expenditures victims undertake to prevent them from being victimized a second time). Some costs are "expected" in advance and thus probabilistic, while others are estimated after a criminal event has already occurred. Finally, some costs are incurred today and others might not accrue until many years into the future. Putting them on an equal footing becomes important for comparison purposes and policy analysis. This section discusses these different definitions and how they relate to our goal of estimating the cost-of-crime. These distinctions become particularly important when conducting policy analysis.

### External costs versus social costs

One of the most confusing and misunderstood concepts in the cost-of-crime literature is the difference between "social costs" and "external costs." Many authors ignore this distinction or otherwise sweep it under the rug, thus making it difficult for the reader to know how to compare different cost estimates. This is not surprising, because there is no real agreement on which crime costs are social costs. Neither is there full agreement on whether or not social costs should be the relevant criteria for assessing the monetary cost or seriousness of crime. Although economists are generally more interested in "social" costs, I argue that the relevant concept for analysis of crime control programs is the concept of "external" costs.

"External costs" are costs imposed by one person on another, where the latter person does not voluntarily accept this negative consequence. For example, the external costs associated with a mugging include stolen property, medical costs, lost wages, as well as pain and suffering endured by the victim. The victim neither asked for, nor voluntarily accepted compensation for enduring, these losses. Moreover, society has deemed that imposing these external costs is morally wrong and against the law.

The concepts of social costs and external costs are closely related but not identical. "Social costs" are costs that reduce the aggregate well-being of society. Although pain and suffering costs are not actual commodities or services exchanged in the marketplace, individuals are willing to pay real dollars and expend real resources in order to avoid the pain, suffering, and lost quality of life associated with becoming a crime victim. Thus, to the extent that society cares about the well-being of crime victims, pain, suffering, and lost quality of life might also be considered social costs of victimization. On the other hand, some might argue that no real resources are lost when a victim endures pain, and that these costs should only be considered "external" costs.

The value of stolen property is also problematic. Some economists have argued that stolen property is an "external" but not technically a "social" cost, since the offender can enjoy the use of the stolen property. For example, Cook (1983: 374) argues that the relevant concept should be the "social cost"—which would exclude transfers of money or property. However, Cook notes that he "presumes that the criminal is properly viewed as a member of society." In contrast, Trumbull (1990) argues that those who violate the criminal law are not entitled to have their utility counted in the social welfare function, i.e. their gain or loss is to be ignored. This example highlights the fact that "social cost" is a normative concept based on a subjective evaluation of whether or not an activity is socially harmful.

Regardless of whether or not one considers stolen property a transfer, there are other social costs associated with theft. Consider the case of an auto theft where the auto is never recovered, but the thief uses the car for his own private benefit. Although technically a "transfer" of property and not a "loss," the fact that those cars are stolen forces potential victims to buy security systems, park in secure lots, and take other preventive measures. If the car or some of its contents are "fenced," resources devoted to the fencing operations are considered social costs, as these resources are diverted from socially productive uses. If the market for fencing operations is competitive, then the resources devoted toward those illicit activities will approximate the value of the stolen merchandise. In a competitive market, the price of the commodity (stolen property sold in the retail market) will equal the marginal cost of production (the cost of resources devoted to the fencing operation). In other words, the value of stolen property might be used as a proxy for these lost resources, and is thus a crude measure of social cost (Becker, 1968: 171, note 3).

Regardless of whether or not stolen property is considered a social cost, society has an interest in enforcing property rights and has determined it is a crime to steal. There will be less productive investment—and therefore less social wealth—in a society where property rights are not enforced. Thus there is certainly some cost associated with a stolen car. For that reason, many economists who study the cost of crime rely on an "external cost" approach, including all costs imposed by a criminal on external parties—whether or not they are technically considered "social costs."

The distinction between social and external costs is most apparent for "victimless crimes" such as drug abuse, prostitution, and gambling. Although economists are often chided for their arguments that these crimes impose no social costs and ought to be legalized, that is a simplistic view of the economic arguments. It is true that there is no direct social cost associated with many of these crimes, since they are voluntarily supplied and demanded, and the individuals who consume these illegal products incur both the direct cost and benefit of these products. However, society has made them illegal for some reason—often because of the collateral consequences that are socially undesirable. Drug abuse imposes many external costs: drug users might be less productive in the workforce and might commit crimes to support their drug habits, dealers might forgo socially productive work activities, society might be burdened with additional medical costs in treating drug addicts.[1] To the extent that these external costs can be identified and measured, they should be included as the cost of victimless crimes.[2] Note that some costs are only "social" costs because society has deemed drug use to be illegal. For example, economists generally consider the forgone legitimate earnings of a person in the illegal drug trade to be a social cost owing to the socially valuable resources that are wasted. However, if society made these drugs legal, those resources would be considered socially productive like any other retail trade activity.

Another complicating factor in conceptualizing social and external costs is the fact that many crimes are allegedly committed as a form of self-help based on the perpetrator's sense of being wronged by the victim (Black,

1998). Examples of this might be an original owner who steals back property that was stolen from him, and assaults committed in response to violent behavior committed by the ultimate victim. Although motives such as revenge or "self-help" do not justify criminal activity, they do raise the question of who is being harmed and whether those harms are "external" or "social" costs society wishes to prevent.

To recap, economists do not agree on the appropriate measure to use when tallying up the costs of crime. Two measures have been proposed—social cost and external cost. The former would exclude such costs as stolen property where the offender's gain is taken into account. The latter would include such transfer costs as long as they involve an illegal activity that deprives one individual of the use of a good that belongs to them without a voluntary transaction taking place. The "external-cost" approach is used throughout this book.

## Tangible versus intangible costs

Although the distinctions are sometimes blurred, we can generally identify two types of cost—tangible and intangible. Tangible costs are those that involve monetary payments such as medical costs, stolen or damaged property, wage losses, prison cells, and police expenditures. These are costs that end up being tallied in the GNP and are normally included in estimates of aggregate or individual wealth.

Intangible or "non-monetary" costs are those not normally exchanged in private or public markets, such as fear, pain, suffering, and lost quality of life. Victims, potential victims, and communities all endure intangible costs of crime. Crime victims endure pain, suffering, and lost quality of life following the physical injury and/or psychological trauma associated with victimization. Potential victims might have increased fear, manifested as psychological anxiety and/or actual averting behavior (e.g. staying home at night, walking longer distances to avoid certain streets).

Later in this chapter we will discuss various methodologies economists have developed to place dollar values on these intangible losses. For now, I want to focus on a more fundamental question: Are these intangible losses really "costs" that should be considered by policymakers when determining the costs and benefits of alternative programs? After all, you cannot "buy" or "sell" pain and suffering in the marketplace. Yet if you asked a victim of a violent crime, they would certainly be willing to pay real money in exchange for not having to endure the pain and suffering victimization. Ask yourself how much you would be willing to pay to avoid being the victim of a serious violent crime. Certainly, this amount would be more than the out-of-pocket losses you would incur. Since people are willing to pay good money to avoid pain and suffering, it must impose a cost on victims when it does occur. Once again, some economists might argue that these are not social costs unless they will involve real resource expenditures such as mental health care or averting behavior. I would prefer to stay away from that debate and instead focus on what I believe to be the more policy-relevant concept of "external costs."

### Direct versus indirect costs

When one offender assaults a victim, the costs to that particular victim can be enumerated and attributed to the offender. I refer to these costs—lost wages, medical expenses, pain, and suffering—as "direct costs," since they are directly caused by the offender. However, there are many more subtle costs that can be attributed to crimes in general and not to any one particular offender. I have termed these "indirect costs," since they cannot be attributed to any one offender. Communities and businesses might suffer from reduced tourism and retail sales as outsiders perceive the community to be a high-crime area. High crime rates might also inhibit economic development as employers and potential employees shun certain communities.

The distinction between direct and indirect costs is not always clear. For example, there is evidence that victims of crime are more likely to move to a new neighborhood following victimization than their non-victim peers. Should the cost of moving be considered a direct cost of victimization? On the one hand, it can be "attributed" to one offender—not to crime in general. On the other hand, one could argue that the decision to move was made by the victim—not the offender. Hence, unlike wage losses, medical costs, and pain and suffering, the costs associated with moving are less direct. I would argue that these moving cost are direct costs attributable to the offender—but only to the extent that one can estimate the increased rate of moving over the background level of moving each year in the population as a whole.[3] Thus it would be difficult if not impossible to attribute any one victim's move to a particular crime. Instead, one might think about a higher probability of moving being associated with each victimization.

### Ex ante *versus* ex post *costs*

Suppose there was a market for pain and suffering where potential offenders who want to inflict harm on another person must negotiate a mutually acceptable price. For some injuries, some people would be willing to accept money in exchange for pain and suffering—if the price were high enough. This price would be the "willingness-to-accept" (WTA) amount for pain and suffering. Suppose, instead, that the potential victim is asked to pay the offender not to inflict harm. In that case, the price would be the "willingness-to-pay" (WTP) amount to avoid pain and suffering. For goods or services that are considered "bad" by consumers, the WTA amount is generally higher than the WTP. This is partly owing to the fact that the WTP amount is based on the wealth of the person being asked to pay, whereas the WTA amount can be unlimited since it is not restricted by the wealth of the person being asked to receive. Indeed, the difference between WTA and WTP is most striking when you consider the prospect of death. Few people would accept less than an infinite amount in exchange for their own death. On the other hand, most people would willingly "pay" their entire wealth in exchange for being saved from an inevitable and immediate death.

Willingness to pay can be thought of as an *ex ante* cost, since people are being asked to pay money in advance. Willingness to accept can be thought of as an *ex post* cost, since the payment takes place after the event actually occurs. This difference is important for policy reasons. If one is interested in examining a proposal to reduce the risk of death to a population, an *ex ante* WTP approach would be the appropriate concept to value, since this is a measure of how much people would themselves be willing to pay to avoid the risk. To pay more would be to waste resources that could go toward more productive activities. Thus the WTP approach is most appropriate for analyzing criminal justice policies or government programs designed to prevent crimes. However, if one is interested in compensating victims of crime for the pain and suffering they actually endured, an *ex post* approach might be more appropriate.

### Opportunity costs

In economics, we consider the "opportunity" cost to be more important than dollars that are actually spent. An opportunity cost is the value of a good or service in its next best alternative. Thus if a victim must spend several hours with police investigators and in court, that victim suffers from a lost opportunity to earn money or to enjoy leisure activities during those hours. Even if, from the employer's perspective, no wages were lost, the victim's opportunity cost of time would be considered a cost imposed by the violent crime. In this particular case, the lost opportunity—generally valued at forgone hourly wages—would be a measure of the opportunity cost of spending time with the criminal justice system.

Similarly, suppose the police budget is fixed and there is one more murder this year compared to last year. The fact that the police force is not expanded in response to this higher crime rate does not mean that this murder resulted in zero police investigation costs. From an opportunity cost standpoint, we should count the time spent by police on investigation—even if no new costs were incurred. In the absence of that new crime, the police could devote their resources to other important activities—including preventing other crimes from occurring. Thus the value of the alternative use of the police resource is the opportunity cost of the additional murder investigation.

### Average versus marginal costs

Oftentimes, a distinction must be made between the average cost and marginal cost of a program. Conceptually, all costs of a crime prevention program should be included in a cost analysis if those costs would not be incurred in the absence of the program. In practice, this requires an understanding of incremental (or marginal) costs versus fixed costs. It also requires an understanding of opportunity costs.

Fixed costs do not vary with the number of participants in the program. Thus the annualized cost associated with maintaining a criminal court (compensation for the judge, debt retirement on the building, etc.) might not be affected by the number of cases actually tried in any year. Other costs—such as a drug rehabilitation program or feeding an incarcerated offender—do vary with the number of participants. These are considered incremental (or marginal) costs. Unless fixed costs change with a policy decision under review, they should be ignored for purposes of assessing that policy.

A cost that is incremental for one decision might be fixed for another. For example, consider the problem of whether or not to increase the average sentence for violent offenders. If prison capacity is not a binding constraint, the incremental costs are primarily the cost of food, medical care, etc. for these offenders. However, if this policy will require additional prison capacity, then the annualized cost of prison cells is part of the incremental costs.

Another important distinction must be made between "marginal" costs and "average" costs imposed by victimization. As discussed above, the marginal costs of victimization include all costs that would not have been incurred in the absence of the victimization. To the victim, they might include medical and wage losses, and fear of future victimization. The latter might manifest itself in many ways such as taking cabs instead of walking, changing jobs, or other forms of 'averting behavior.' However, the fact that many non-victimized citizens have an increased fear of crime resulting from an increase in the rate of violence cannot be attributed to any single victimization. Put differently, eliminating one violent act will not reduce the public's fear of crime. Thus these costs might be excluded from the "marginal cost" of any one crime. On the other hand, to ignore these costs would be to underestimate the true costs of crime. This distinction is important, as many of the costs of crime and drug abuse are of this more aggregate nature. Thus a comprehensive analysis of the aggregate cost of crime should include these cost categories. Of course, if an intervention program is designed to attack a large enough percentage of the population of violent offenders, it might ultimately affect some of these larger social problems. Thus, on a larger scale, the aggregate benefits of programs designed to reduce violence might exceed the sum of the benefits of individual programs.[4]

Note that when estimating the cost of incarceration (or savings owing to less incarceration), whether or not the annualized cost of constructing a prison cell should be included depends crucially on the capacity constraint. If there are empty beds, the "opportunity cost" of the prison cell is zero, and the only cost is food, electricity, medical care, etc. for the additional prisoner. In that case, the cost of the prison space itself is a "sunk" cost that is not relevant to the costs and benefits of the proposal under consideration. The financing cost of the prison will be incurred regardless of whether or not another drug abuser is incarcerated, thus there will be no "savings" from diverting the drug abuser to a non-incarcerative treatment program. On the other hand, if the prison is operating at full capacity and lack of prison space was forcing authorities to incarcerate fewer individuals than they would otherwise, the annualized cost of the prison cell might be considered an "opportunity cost" that is saved by diverting the offender. In that case, money is indeed being saved by not having to build another cell and/or by not enduring a higher crime rate owing to the inability to incarcerate other offenders.

A final point of some importance is that marginal costs are not necessarily constant. Instead, they vary considerably as the quantity of crime varies. This is particularly true for many of the indirect costs of crime. For example, consider a world where there were no crimes at all. We would expect very little expenditure on security alarms or other prevention devices. Neighborhoods would not suffer the declining value that some high-crime areas currently endure. However, if one rapist suddenly appeared in a neighborhood, the indirect costs associated with that rapist might be enormous—as people dramatically changed their everyday behavior, bought security alarms, etc. Thus the cost of that first rape is enormous, and each additional rape in the community will likely also be quite high as more and more people take such precautions. However, after some point, one additional rape will add little to these indirect costs as most people have taken precautions and they are now accustomed to a higher risk of crime. Of course, this does not reduce the direct costs associated with each rape. Another reason why the marginal costs of victimization may not be constant is due to what economists call the "wealth effect." For example if someone is willing to spend $1,000 to reduce the risk of a rape occurring, they might not be willing to spend their second $1,000 for a further reduction. The reason for this is that the second $1,000 is being requested in the context of already having $1,000 less in disposable income. Whereas the first $1,000 might divert funds that would otherwise go for entertainment, for example, the next $1,000 might involve more difficult trade-offs in terms of that person's household budget.

## Victim assistance and other cost-reducing investments

Some of the costs associated with crime may actually be designed to reduce the cost of victimization. For example, victim service agencies provide a variety of psychological treatment programs for victims and assist victims in dealing with the judicial process. At first, it might seem that it is simply inappropriate to include these as a cost of victimization. After all, victim service agencies really provide a social benefit. However, in the absence of these victim service agencies, the costs of victimization would be even higher—as the pain and suffering endured by crime victims would increase.

Averting expenditures such as alarms, defensive weapons, and behavioral changes are also a form of cost-reducing investment that can be attributed to the indirect costs of crimes.

## From whose perspective are costs to be measured?

One of the most significant costs of crime is the pain, suffering, and lost quality of life suffered by victims. Economists have long noted that "psychic" benefits and costs are part of individual utility and hence social welfare. Individuals are willing to trade off tangible goods and services in exchange for some of these psychic benefits. Thus, as discussed earlier, they represent real social costs and benefits. Similarly, individuals who suffer the pain, suffering, and lost quality of life through becoming a crime victim would be willing to pay real dollars to reduce those psychic costs.

Although lost productivity of incarcerated offenders is normally included in estimates of the cost of crime, noticeably missing is the lost quality of life to offenders while behind bars. When an offender is locked up and unable to be gainfully employed, not only does the offender lose wages, but society loses the value of those hours of work. Hence the offender's lost productivity is often included by economists as both a social and an external cost. However, the pain, suffering, and lost quality of life of the offender in prison is not considered either an external or a social cost of crime, since the offender is the only one who suffers. Not all would agree with this approach, however, as anti-prison activists might care very much about the treatment of imprisoned offenders. They might also care about the monetary and psychic costs to the family of the offender. The latter are more properly considered both external and social costs, to the extent that the family of the offender did not participate in the crime. As this example illustrates, benefit–cost analysis is not a value-free concept, but instead involves definitions and explicit boundaries in order to determine whose costs and benefits matter.

Another common issue in determining whose costs and benefits should be considered arises when policymakers conduct cost–benefit analyses. Policy analysts are often more concerned with taxpayer implications than they are with the "social" or "external" cost implications. Thus a cost–benefit analysis of a criminal justice program will often compare the costs and benefits to taxpayers. This approach might ignore such important costs and benefits as the victim's well-being or the safety of the community as a whole. In other words, decisions might be made that alleviate the burden facing taxpayers— but at the expense of crime victims or other members of the public.

### Timing of costs and discounting to present value

An injury that is sustained today may continue to have consequences and impose costs for many years. Thus, if one is interested in the cost of crime in any one year, it is important to decide whether this should be defined as the costs actually incurred during that year ("prevalence"-based costs), or the costs imposed that year even if they are not realized until many years down the road ("incidence"-based costs). Cost estimates based on incidence count both present and future costs in the year in which the injury-cost stream began (Hartunian, Smart, and Thompson, 1981). Costs based on prevalence count all costs of injury that were incurred in a given year, regardless of when the injuries occurred.[5] Incidence-based estimates indicate how much could be saved by preventing future incidents and are thus most relevant for criminal justice policy analysis. Prevalence-based estimates may be used to provide insight into the cost savings attainable through improved treatment of existing injuries and are of more interest to those in the public health community interested in estimating medical care needs.

Since our purpose is largely to inform criminal justice policy, and not to be solely concerned with short-term medical care needs, the costs in this book and in most studies of the cost of crime are "incidence" estimates. They include all present and future costs associated with individual victim-izations. Costs incurred in the future (i.e. more than one year post-victimization) must be discounted to "present value." Since a dollar spent today is not the same as a dollar spent 15 years from now, future costs must be discounted to present value when compared to the costs borne today.[6] Although there is no general consensus on the appropriate discount rate for purposes of policy analysis, most "cost-of-crime" studies have used a rate of between 2 percent and 3 percent per year, which is consistent with the "real" (i.e. net of inflation) discount rate for worker wages over time, and the real consumer interest rate over time.[7] This discount rate is also within the range most likely to be used in tort awards for lost wages. Further, statistical mod-eling suggests workers apply a 2 percent discount rate when they trade off possible loss of future life years against extra earnings in the present (Moore and Viscusi, 1989). Finally, the Congressional Budget Office concluded from a review of the economic evidence that the most appropriate discount rate for public decisionmaking was 2 percent (Hartman, 1990). A similar con-sensus appears to have developed around a 3 percent net discount rate in health care economics (Gold, 1996). Some government agencies, however, have routinely used net discount rates of around 10 percent, and the Office of Management and Budget (1992) only recently reduced its required dis-count rate for regulatory policy analysis to 7 percent.

The higher the discount rate the lower the present value of future benefits. The choice of a proper discount rate is especially important in con-sidering the benefits of youth prevention programs or other programs whose crime reduction benefits might not accrue for many years. Although this issue is nowhere near being settled, it is less of a problem in the criminal justice context than in environmental issues—where it is common for latency periods to extend 20, 30, or 40 years or more (see Revesz, 1999).

## Methodologies for estimating costs

There are many different approaches to measuring the costs of crime. Broadly, these methods can be described as either "direct" or "indirect." Direct methods use primary sources such as crime-victim surveys or budgets of the criminal justice system. Indirect methods use secondary sources such as property values or jury awards. This section reviews the state of the art in identifying and measuring both the tangible and intangible costs of crime.

### Tangible costs of crime

At first it might appear that the tangible costs of crime are relatively straightforward to estimate. In fact, aside from data on direct government expenditures on the criminal justice system, this is far from the truth. For example, there is no national accounting system tallying up the out-of-pocket losses to crime victims. The only direct source of crime-victim costs is the ongoing National Crime Victimization Survey (NCVS), which interviews households and elicits information from those who have experienced a recent criminal victimization (Bureau of Justice Statistics, 2003a). The NCVS includes several questions asking crime victims about their out-of-pocket losses, including an estimate of the dollar cost of medical care, lost wages, and property loss. These estimates are periodically published by the Bureau of Justice Statistics (see e.g. Klaus, 1994).

Despite their official-looking stature, the NCVS crime-cost estimates severely understate the tangible costs of crime to victims. First, for the NCVS, the reference period for crimes committed is the previous six months. Since the average crime will have occurred about three months prior to its being reported to the NCVS, any medical costs or lost wages are necessarily limited to those short-term costs. Even short-term costs are likely to be underestimated, however, since hospital bills are often sent directly to insurance companies, and may arrive months after hospitalization. Second, some cost categories are simply excluded from the NCVS. For example, respondents are not asked about mental health care, despite the fact that this is a significant cost of victimization (Cohen and Miller, 1998). In addition, the consequences of victimization can be far-reaching and beyond the scope of any government survey. Although few studies have quantified these effects, a recent study by Dugan (1999) found that victims were more likely to move to a new home following victimization than their peers who were not victimized. The long-term implications of victimization may also be hidden and underestimated. For example, a recent study by Macmillan (2000) finds that educational attainment and lifetime earnings are lower for victims of childhood physical or sexual assault. These impacts have yet to be incorporated into cost-of-crime estimates that are based on victim costs.

Other tangible crime costs that are relatively easier to measure include police expenditures and the criminal justice system itself. Although aggregate costs may be available from government statistics, the cost per crime is not always available. For some purposes, we might be interested in these costs. For example, in studying the costs and benefits of an early-release program, we would want to know the cost of recidivism imposed by those who are let out of prison early. Thus we might want the marginal cost of police resources associated with investigating a crime, as well as the marginal costs to the criminal justice system from having to reprocess a repeat offender. Such studies exist for specific jurisdictions and/or specific time frames. However, these studies are not routinely updated and the costs might vary considerably by location.

Finally, even potential victims suffer tangible costs of crime by taking costly preventive measures—such as purchasing and installing security systems, deadbolt locks, cell phones, guard dogs, and guns purchased for defensive protection. Although direct measures of these expenditures should be relatively easy to obtain through survey methods, one difficulty in doing so is the fact that many of these expenditures serve dual roles. The guard dog may also be a pet that provides companionship. The cell phone might provide a sense of security to a nighttime traveler, but also can be used for other purposes. Sorting out the reason for purchase and value obtained for each reason is not a trivial task.

## Intangible costs of crime

Several different approaches have been utilized to estimate the monetary value of intangible costs. Perhaps the earliest indirect method was to infer property owners' willingness to pay for a safer neighborhood through higher property values. To the extent that home buyers take into account the risk of victimization when deciding whether or not to buy a home, we expect higher-crime neighborhoods to have lower housing prices controlling for all other factors that affect house prices (Thaler, 1978). A statistical methodology called "hedonic pricing" has been developed to estimate the component of the housing price that is attributable to crime. The methodology developed by Thaler (1978) requires detailed location-specific housing characteristics (square feet, number of rooms, age, etc.), housing prices, crime rates, and other location-specific amenities (e.g, tax rates, school quality, distance to center city, etc.). Statistical techniques (e.g. multiple regression analysis) isolate the effect of crime on housing prices. The effect that crime has on housing prices can be inferred from this statistical technique (e.g. from the regression coefficient on the crime variable), and one can interpret this relationship as the marginal willingness to pay for a reduction in the crime rate. Note that this is a marginal valuation, based on the current crime rate and small changes around that rate.

Property value studies necessarily rely on important assumptions about the competitiveness of the housing market and consumer information about neighborhood crime rates. They also ignore the effect that location-specific amenities—including crime—have on local wage rates. A few researchers have estimated both a housing and a wage equation in order to capture both effects (see e.g. Hoehn, Berger, and Blomquist, 1987). Although these researchers estimate two equations, they have yet to estimate simultaneous models taking account of the interaction between housing prices and wages.

Data limitations have generally prevented these property value and/or wage rate studies from isolating the cost of any individual crime type. Since many types of crime tend to move in similar directions, it is difficult to sort out the effect that one particular crime has on wage rates or property values. Instead, studies to date have estimated the cost of an aggregate measure of crime such as the crime index. In theory, a comprehensive data set could isolate the effect of each crime type on housing prices. A recent study by Bartley (2000) had some success in isolating these costs by analyzing wages and rents in cities around the country. However, even larger data sets and more fine geographic distinctions appear to be needed to fully disentangle these individual crime costs.

One of the positive features of the property value studies of crime is that they rely upon actual market transactions. Although economists tend to favor estimation procedures whereby actual market transactions (e.g. housing prices) are used, any market-based approach necessarily takes into account the wealth and income of the buyer. Thus the fact that less wealthy individuals necessarily buy less expensive homes leads to an estimate of the value of crime that is based on "ability to pay." This issue will reappear several times in this chapter, since many of the methodologies discussed here will depend on the income of the victim or potential victim. In some cases, researchers or policymakers who want to impose a different value system can easily adjust the estimates to "neutralize" the effect of ability to pay and instead estimate the willingness to pay for a "typical" citizen. However, this cannot be done in all cases.

The housing market is not the only place affected by crime rates. People buy handguns and security alarms and take cabs instead of walking, and other precautions are taken to avoid crime. Although all of these expenditures can be considered part of the cost of society's response to crime, they might also be used in estimating the cost of crime itself. For example, a study of the purchase of security alarms might allow us to infer the value that consumers place on a particular reduction in the probability of being victimized. Thus if the purchase of a double-bolt lock at the cost of $25 reduces the risk of being burglarized from one in 500 to one in 1,000, we could infer that the individual who purchases the lock values the reduced risk by at least that amount. Collectively, if 1,000 households were willing to pay $25 to decrease their risk from two in 1,000 to one in 1,000 (hence preventing one burglary from occurring among this population of 1,000 individuals), this would imply a willingness to pay of $25,000 to reduce one burglary ($25 × 1,000 = $25,000).

Another method of estimating the non-monetary costs of crime is to infer society's willingness to pay for reductions in crime from non-crime studies of society's willingness to pay for safety. Although there are several approaches, this growing literature primarily estimates wage rate differentials for risky jobs (Viscusi, 1998 and 2000). Thus, for example, if workers are paid an additional $50 wage rate premium for accepting an increased risk of death of one in 500,000, that is interpreted to mean that the collective "value of life" is $25 million ($50 × 500,000). There is now an extensive literature on the statistical "value of life." Value-of-life estimates should not be interpreted as the value of any one particular life but, instead, as society's value of saving a "statistical" life. The first attempt to incorporate these "value-of-life" estimates into the cost of crime appears to be Phillips and Votey (1981), who combined the "value-of-life" estimates and out-of-pocket costs of crime with society's perception of the seriousness of crime to arrive at crime-specific monetary estimates. However, their methodology was unable to account for the risk of injury and death for many crimes.

Cohen (1988a) attempted to overcome these data limitations by combining estimates of the "value of life" with monetary estimates of the pain, suffering, and lost quality of life for non-fatal injuries. The approach used in Cohen (1988a) is a hybrid of direct- and indirect-cost estimation. Direct costs are taken from NCVS data as well as several additional sources to augment some of the weaknesses of the government survey. Non-monetary costs are estimated using indirect techniques. The value-of-life estimates were used to value the risk of being fatally injured during the commission of a crime. These include the "value of life" for fatal crimes and pain, suffering, and lost quality of life for non-fatal injuries. Risk of death is calculated directly from FBI data identifying the underlying crime in homicide cases. Risk-of-death probabilities are multiplied by the "value of life" to arrive at an estimate of the value of the risk of death component of each crime type.

The innovative—and most controversial—methodology introduced by Cohen (1988a) was the use of jury award data to estimate the monetary value of pain, suffering, and lost quality of life for non-fatal injuries. At the time, Cohen (1988a) relied upon jury awards in traditional tort cases and matched up the type and severity of injury (e.g. broken bones) found in tort cases with typical injuries identified in crime victim data through the NCVS. This approach implicitly assumes that identical injuries are valued the same whether caused by an auto accident or an assault. However, crime victims might endure more pain and suffering owing to the psychological trauma and fear of repeat victimization. More recently, Miller, Cohen, and Wiersema (1996) obtained data on jury awards to victims of physical and sexual assault and estimated crime costs using these court cases. These data were unavailable previously, since civil lawsuits by crime victims are a relatively new phenomenon that has grown to the point where adequate data exist. These lawsuits are generally against third parties for inadequate security, such as a parking lot owner that did not provide adequate lighting or an apartment owner that did not adequately secure a building.

One reason the jury award approach is controversial is the popular notion that jury awards in the U.S. are unpredictable and/or unreasonably high. Despite popular beliefs to the contrary, considerable evidence exists that jury awards are predictable in a large sample (Cohen and Miller, 2003). In addition, Cohen and Miller (2003) found that the implied statistical value of life awarded by juries is very comparable to that found in studies of worker wage rate differentials. Popular press articles and calls for tort reform often focus on the outliers and punitive damage awards. Punitive damages are meant to punish the tortfeasor, not to compensate the victim; hence they are excluded from the pain, suffering, and lost quality-of-life estimates. Compensatory damages (i.e. payments that are meant to compensate for out-of-pocket and pain and suffering, but not to punish), however, are quite predictable, and jury awards are being used as a measure of pain and suffering in other contexts, including government regulatory agencies (e.g. the Consumer Product Safety Commission). Perhaps most compelling, however, is the fact that our society has placed its tort system in the hands of juries and has decided that these awards are "just compensation."

Despite my defense of the use of jury awards to measure victim compensation for non-monetary harms, this approach is theoretically not the most appropriate for purposes of estimating the willingness to pay to reduce the risk of crime. Jury awards are *ex post* compensation designed to make a person whole. In fact, no amount of money will really make a person "whole." How many murder victims do you think would have accepted a $2 million payment in exchange for their life? Thus the measure that we really want for determining public policy outcomes is based on the risk of victimization. We are all willing to trade off money for small changes in the risk of injury or death—we do it all of the time in our everyday activities by deciding whether or not to purchase a less safe car or a burglar alarm, or to take a cab at night instead of walking in an unsafe neighborhood. As discussed in the previous section, for policy purposes the more relevant question is the "willingness to pay" (WTP) to reduce crime, which is an *ex ante* concept. The *ex post* compensation approach necessarily overstates the amount the public would be willing to pay to reduce the impact of crime on victims. The property value studies described above are *ex ante* WTP approaches, since they are based on actual market transactions taking into account the prospective risk of criminal victimization. However, as noted earlier, researchers have only been able to value an index crime using this method—not individual crime types.[8]

An alternative approach to estimating the *ex ante* WTP for reduced crime is to directly survey the public (i.e. potential victims). This approach, often called "contingent valuation," is a methodology developed in the environmental economics literature and has been used extensively to place dollar values on non-market goods such as improvements in air quality or endangered species. There have been literally hundreds of contingent valuation studies, meta-analyses and textbooks written on the subject.[9] Although

there is some disagreement on the reliability of these surveys, they are continually being used in benefit–cost analysis and natural resource damages
litigation, and for other purposes. A distinguished panel of social scientists,
chaired by two Nobel laureates in economics (Arrow *et al.*, 1993) were
commissioned by the National Oceanic and Atmospheric Administration
(NOAA) to assess the contingent valuation methodology. This panel was
brought together because NOAA had drafted regulations calling for the use
of this methodology when estimating natural resource damages in legal proceedings involving compensation for damaged public property. The panel
concluded that this is a valid approach and provided a set of guidelines for
conducting a reliable contingent valuation survey. Thus, if done properly,
contingent valuation surveys can be useful policy tools. Although being used
in many different policy contexts, contingent valuation is only beginning to
be employed in criminal justice research (see Cohen *et al.*, 2004).

---

### "Pain and suffering" versus "lost quality of life"

Although there is a conceptual difference between "pain and suffering" and "quality-of-life" costs to victims, the distinction can sometimes become blurred. Pain and suffering is a monetized value of the
physical and mental pain and anguish endured by the victim owing to
the injury. Quality-of-life costs involve the monetization of enjoyable
activities the victim is no longer able to undertake as a result of the
injury. For example, a rape victim's pain and suffering might be
thought of as the mental and physical damage caused by the rape,
whereas the loss in quality of life might be owing to activities the
victim no longer feels safe undertaking, such as taking walks in the
park.

Although we can conceptualize these differences, it is virtually
impossible to separate them out empirically. Willingness-to-pay studies
are unable to distinguish between these two costs, as they look at how
consumers or workers value additional risk in general—not any one
component of risk. It may be possible in the future to distinguish these
costs using the *ex post* compensation approach, as juries in some states
are beginning to specify each component of compensation separately.
However, courts are just beginning to recognize "loss of enjoyment" as
a distinct category from "pain and suffering." It is not clear whether
this distinction will result in increased average awards or if juries currently include their valuation of lost quality of life when making pain
and suffering awards.

Throughout this book, the terms "pain and suffering" and "quality
of life" are generally assumed to be interchangeable. Further, we will
not distinguish between them in making cost estimates.

Finally, economists often rely upon indirect measurement techniques by appealing to the notions of opportunity cost and revealed preference. In some instances, this is as straightforward as identifying forgone productive opportunities, such as the time an offender spends in prison, or the time a victim spends out of work while dealing with the criminal justice process. In other instances, the costs are much more subtle. If consumers are rational and act in their own self-interest (in the jargon of economics, are "utility maximizers"), we can learn many useful things from their behavior—e.g., their "revealed preference" for one choice over another. Thus the fact that individuals choose a leisure activity over working another hour provides us with a lower-bound estimate of the value of that leisure activity—it must be at least as much as the opportunity cost of the time involved. Put differently, if an individual enjoys an hour of leisure time instead of working overtime and earning $30 per hour, we can infer that the person values his/her own time by at least that amount. This notion can be used to value the cost of many preventive or avoidance activities that people take to reduce their likelihood of victimization. Examples of these time costs include the time people take to lock and unlock cars and homes and taking a longer route home to avoid a bad neighborhood.

Some crimes with very large intangible costs, like treason or crimes that betray the public trust, may never be monetized. However, that does not invalidate the theory that would identify the social cost of treason to be the risk of harm to our national security or the social cost of a public betrayal of trust to be a diminution of public trust and moral behavior.

## Criticisms of the cost-of-crime literature

Although few would disagree with the fact that enumerating victim costs is a worthwhile exercise, there is less agreement on whether costs should be measured. For example, Zimring and Hawkins (1995) are highly critical of recent attempts to monetize the cost of crime. They argue that the "state of the art" in economics has not developed to the point where we can adequately characterize the social costs and benefits—either in theory or in practice. Zimring and Hawkins argue that economists have problems both in defining the social cost of crime and in measuring it in any meaningful way. Although there is some validity to both concerns, there is also much confusion about the proper role benefit–cost analysis can play in policy debates. In Chapter 5, I will discuss benefit–cost analysis, its proper use, and its limitations. Here, I address the theoretical concerns that Zimring and Hawkins express about the problem of defining costs.

Zimring and Hawkins note that recent attempts to estimate the monetary costs of crime fail to articulate a coherent theory underlying their cost estimates. Part of the problem is a misunderstanding of the difference between social costs and external costs, a subject that was discussed at length above. As an example, Zimring and Hawkins (1995: 141) cite the theft of a $50,000

Mercedes whose owner failed to take relatively inexpensive antitheft precautions. Noting that this might be a $50,000 personal loss to the owner, they wonder what the social cost is. As discussed earlier, although there might be some disagreement about whether the $50,000 theft is technically a "social cost," there is no doubt that it is an "external cost" that society has an interest in preventing. Since society has laws making it a crime to involuntarily appropriate the property of others, and the harm to the victim is clearly related to the value of the item stolen, $50,000 is a good estimate of the external cost of the crime.

Next, Zimring and Hawkins raise the concern that "any public expenditure to prevent it up to $49,999 would be justified on a cost–benefit basis." This is where Zimring and Hawkins's analysis is flawed. On the contrary, I would not argue that society should spend up to $49,999 to prevent this theft. This would be an improper application of benefit–cost analysis. Although a simple comparison of the external cost of the theft to a proposal requiring an expenditure of $49,999 to prevent the theft would conclude that benefits exceed costs, a thorough benefit–cost analysis must consider alternative policies. If alternative measures could prevent the theft at a lower cost, those alternatives would be preferred and they would be economically efficient. To spend $49,999 to prevent a theft that could be prevented for $200 is economically inefficient. Moreover, there is no reason that society must spend $200 to prevent a theft that the owner of a Mercedes can prevent himself for $200.

This example has two important policy implications. First, it is not appropriate to examine only one policy option. Instead, policy analysts should examine many alternatives to find the one that has the highest benefit–cost ratio or the most "bang for your buck." Indeed, regulatory agencies are often required by law to consider all technically feasible alternatives to proposed regulations. Second, there is no reason that society has to spend money to protect the property of an individual who is wealthy and has the means to offer the same private protection. Indeed, economic theory would tell us that it is inefficient for the government to intervene unless it costs less for the government to provide the protection than it does for private parties. However, unless there are serious third-party effects, or other "social costs," the fact that someone in society suffers an "external cost" is not necessarily sufficient grounds for government intervention.

Zimring and Hawkins raise another objection to the use of "cost-of-crime" estimates that include intangible costs such as pain, suffering, and lost quality of life. They note, for example, that the intangible cost of a murder has been estimated by Cohen (1988a) to be approximately $2 million. If all deaths in the United States were valued at that level, they note, the "cost" of all deaths in the U.S. would exceed the gross national product. Following their logic, if one uses intangible costs to determine how much society should spend to prevent a social ill such as crime, we should be willing to spend our entire wealth on preventing death and ignore all other aspects of life. The fallacy in this line of thinking, however, is forgetting the fact that for policy purposes, these estimates are only of value in making marginal decisions. In other words, they can be used to compare the benefits and costs of a particular policy proposal that will have a relatively small impact on crime and do not have a significant "wealth" effect on society. Thus if we were to spend hundreds of billions of dollars more fighting crime, the marginal benefit of crime control would decrease dramatically relative to the benefit of placing attention on other social ills. Thus the real concern raised by the Zimring and Hawkins critique is that for policy purposes, we must keep in mind that cost estimates are being made based on current levels of crime and current levels of health and well-being, and that (as noted above) the marginal cost of crime is not constant.

# 3    Victim costs

The most direct impact of crime is borne by victims. Despite this fact, victims have often been the least studied and least organized, and have the least input into the criminal justice process. Prior to the mid-1980s, it was generally believed that the cost of the criminal justice system dwarfed the cost imposed on victims. However, once economists began to include the intangible costs of crime such as pain, suffering, and lost quality of life, this relationship has reversed itself. Victim costs are now seen to be the largest component of the cost of crime. At the same time, victim rights have become more important in the criminal justice system, as have victim rights organizations. This chapter focuses on victim costs—both tangible and intangible. In addition to adding these costs up, we briefly look at the demographics of victimization (i.e. who suffers the most) and attempts to compensate victims for the costs they bear. Most of this chapter deals with traditional "street crime." However, we also consider two important areas of crime that impose significant social costs: (1) economic crimes such as fraud, anti-trust, and crimes against the environment, and (2) drug crimes.

Table 3.1 (overleaf) lists the major crime categories and the average costs for victims of most types of violent and property crime in the U.S. It is taken from the most recent U.S. estimates of the cost of crime to victims—Miller, Cohen, and Wiersema (1996). Note that the costs shown in Table 3.1 include both tangible and intangible costs, and are averaged over both completed and attempted crimes. This chapter will enumerate the crime cost categories that go into these estimates—including lost wages/productivity, medical care, mental health care, police and fire services, victim services, property losses, and pain, suffering, and lost quality of life. Costs generally borne by third parties or society as a whole are reserved for Chapter 4.

The costs in Table 3.1 are based on "victimizations," not "victims." Thus if a victim is subjected to repeated victimizations, each one is estimated as a separate event. It is possible, for example, that the psychological trauma associated with a repeat victimization is worse than twice that of a single victimization. If so, these figures would need to be adjusted upward to account for repeat victimizations. On the other hand, if the psychological trauma associated with repeat victimization is less than the sum of individual single-event victimizations, these figures would be too high.

*Table 3.1* Dollar losses per criminal victimization (including attempts)

| | Productivity ($) | Medical care/ ambulance ($) | Mental health care ($) | Police/ fire services ($) |
|---|---|---|---|---|
| *Fatal crime* | | | | |
| Rape, assault, etc. | 1,000,000 | 16,300 | 4,800 | 1,300 |
| Arson deaths | 724,000 | 17,600 | 4,800 | 1,900 |
| DWI | 1,150,000 | 18,300 | 4,800 | 740 |
| *Child abuse* | 2,200 | 430 | 2,500 | 29 |
| Sexual abuse (incl. rape) | 2,100 | 490 | 5,800 | 56 |
| Physical abuse | 3,400 | 790 | 2,700 | 20 |
| Emotional abuse | 900 | 0 | 2,700 | 20 |
| *Rape and sexual assault (excluding child abuse)* | 2,200 | 500 | 2,200 | 37 |
| *Other assault or attempt* | 950 | 425 | 76 | 60 |
| NCVS with injury | 3,100 | 1,470 | 97 | 84 |
| Age 0–11 with injury | 2,800 | 1,470 | 100 | 84 |
| Non-NCVS domestic | 760 | 310 | 81 | 0 |
| No injury | 70 | 0 | 65 | 69 |
| *Robbery or attempt* | 950 | 370 | 66 | 130 |
| With injury | 2,500 | 1,000 | 65 | 160 |
| No injury | 75 | 0 | 66 | 110 |
| *Drunk-driving* | 2,800 | 1,400 | 82 | 40 |
| With injury | 12,100 | 6,400 | 82 | 120 |
| No injury | 170 | 0 | 82 | 17 |
| *Arson* | 1,750 | 1,100 | 18 | 1,000 |
| With injury | 15,400 | 10,000 | 24 | 1,000 |
| No injury | 8 | 0 | 18 | 1,000 |
| *Larceny or attempt* | 8 | 0 | 6 | 80 |
| *Burglary or attempt* | 12 | 0 | 5 | 130 |
| *Motor vehicle theft or attempt* | 45 | 0 | 5 | 140 |

Source: Miller, Cohen, and Wiersema (1996), Table 2.

*Notes*
All estimates in 1993 dollars. Totals may not add owing to rounding. Major categories are in italics, subcategories listed under italic headings. ? = unknown.

Table 3.2 (on p. 44) summarizes the total costs from Table 3.1 by re-calculating the figures in several different ways. The first column is the same as Table 3.1, where costs are on a "per-victimization" basis. The second column is also on a per-victimization basis. However, this approach now includes a "risk of death" component. In many circumstances, murder occurs as the end result of a less severe underlying crime. Thus, for example,

Table 3.1 (continued)

| Social/ victim services ($) | Property loss/damage ($) | Subtotal: tangible losses ($) | Quality of life ($) | Total ($) |
|---|---|---|---|---|
| 0 | 120 | 1,030,000 | 1,910,000 | 2,940,000 |
| 0 | 21,600 | 770,000 | 1,970,000 | 2,740,000 |
| 0 | 9,700 | 1,180,000 | 1,995,000 | 3,180,000 |
| 1,800 | 10 | 7,931 | 52,371 | 60,000 |
| 1,100 | 0 | 9,500 | 89,800 | 99,000 |
| 2,100 | 26 | 9,000 | 57,500 | 67,000 |
| 2,100 | 0 | 5,700 | 21,100 | 2,700 |
| 27 | 100 | 5,100 | 81,400 | 87,000 |
| 16 | 26 | 1,550 | 7,800 | 9,400 |
| 46 | 39 | 4,800 | 19,300 | 24,000 |
| 46 | 39 | 4,600 | 28,100 | 33,000 |
| 0 | 39 | 1,200 | 10,000 | 11,000 |
| 9 | 15 | 200 | 1,700 | 2,000 |
| 25 | 750 | 2,300 | 5,700 | 8,000 |
| 44 | 1,400 | 5,200 | 13,800 | 19,000 |
| 15 | 400 | 700 | 1,3000 | 2,000 |
| ? | 1,600 | 6,000 | 11,900 | 18,000 |
| ? | 3,600 | 22,300 | 48,400 | 71,000 |
| 0 | 1,000 | 1,300 | 1,400 | 2,700 |
| ? | 15,500 | 19,500 | 18,000 | 37,500 |
| ? | 22,400 | 49,000 | 153,000 | 202,000 |
| 0 | 14,600 | 16,000 | 500 | 16,000 |
| 1 | 270 | 370 | 0 | 370 |
| 5 | 970 | 1,100 | 300 | 1,400 |
| 0 | 3,300 | 3,500 | 300 | 3,700 |

one can estimate the "risk of murder" from a rape and include the monetary value of that risk in the estimate of the cost of rape. Presumably, by reducing the underlying crime we also reduce the risk of murder. This approach is discussed in detail later in the chapter. The third and fourth columns in Table 3.2 switch the unit of analysis to "per victim." Thus it accounts for the fact that some of the victimizations in the earlier columns are perpetrated

*Table 3.2* Crime severity measured by monetized losses per crime victimization or per crime victim (in 1993 dollars)

| | Per victimization | | Per victim | |
|---|---|---|---|---|
| | w/o risk of death ($) | w/risk of death ($) | w/o risk of death ($) | w/risk of death ($) |
| Child abuse: sexual | 99,000 | * | 125,000 | * |
| Rape and sexual assault (excluding child abuse) | 87,000 | 87,000 | 109,000 | 110,000 |
| Child abuse: physical | 67,000 | * | 77,000 | * |
| Child abuse (all types) | 60,000 | 63,000 | 70,000 | 74,000 |
| Arson | 38,000 | 54,000 | 38,000 | 54,000 |
| Child abuse: emotional | 27,000 | * | 30,000 | * |
| Drunk-driving | 18,000 | 26,000 | 18,000 | 26,000 |
| Assault or attempt (NCVS) | 9,000 | 19,000 | 12,000 | 31,000 |
| Assault (any) | 9,000 | 15,000 | 14,000 | 23,000 |
| Robbery or attempt | 8,000 | 13,000 | 10,000 | 16,000 |
| Motor vehicle theft | 4,000 | 4,000 | 4,000 | 4,000 |
| Burglary | 1,400 | 1,500 | 1,600 | 1,700 |
| Larceny | 370 | 370 | 400 | 400 |

Source: Miller, Cohen, and Wiersema (1996).

Notes
1 Assault, robbery, motor vehicle theft, burglary, and larceny include "attempted" crimes that are never successfully carried out. If the other crime categories excluded attempts, the arson and drunk-driving categories might drop in the rankings. See text.

* Deaths owing to child abuse are not categorized by type of child abuse (e.g., sexual, physical, or emotional). Thus the estimates do not include the risk of death. However, a combined child abuse category is included in this table, which includes the risk-of-death estimate.

against the same individual. As noted above, this approach uses a simple extrapolation, by assuming that each additional victimization is exactly as costly to the victim as the first.

Clearly, the cost of a murder or other crime that results in death (e.g. fatal arsons or drunk driving fatalities) dwarfs other crime categories, at about $3 million per victim. As shown in Table 3.2, the second most costly crime on a per-victimization basis is child sexual abuse ($99,000), followed by rape ($87,000), child physical abuse ($67,000), and arson ($38,000). The figures for assault, rape, robbery, motor vehicle theft, burglary, and larceny all include "attempted" crimes that are never successfully carried out. If the other crime categories excluded unsuccessful attempts, the arson and drunk-driving categories might drop in the rankings, since there is no way to account for "attempted" crimes for these categories.

Table 3.3 tallies up the cost per victimization by the number of victimizations in the U.S. The individual cost categories in Table 3.3 exclude the "risk of death," since all deaths are included in the "fatal crimes" category. To

*Table 3.3* Aggregate annual costs of criminal victimization (millions of 1993 dollars)

| | Tangible ($m) | Quality of life ($m) | Total ($m) |
|---|---|---|---|
| *Fatal crime (1990)* | 33,000 | 60,000 | 93,000 |
| Rape/robbery/abuse/neglect/assault | 25,000 | 46,000 | 71,000 |
| Arson deaths | 600 | 1,700 | 2,000 |
| Drunk-driving deaths (DWI) | 7,200 | 12,300 | 20,000 |
| *Child abuse* | 7,300 | 48,000 | 56,000 |
| Rape | 900 | 8,000 | 9,000 |
| Sexual abuse | 1,400 | 12,800 | 14,000 |
| Physical abuse | 3,200 | 20,400 | 24,000 |
| Emotional abuse | 1,900 | 7,100 | 9,000 |
| *Rape and sexual abuse (adult)* | 7,500 | 119,000 | 127,000 |
| *Other assault or attempt* | 15,000 | 77,000 | 93,000 |
| NCVS with injury | 11,000 | 44,900 | 56,000 |
| Age 0–11 with injury | 600 | 3,900 | 5,000 |
| Non-NCVS domestic | 2,200 | 19,100 | 21,000 |
| No injury | 1,300 | 9,500 | 11,000 |
| *Robbery or attempt* | 3,100 | 8,000 | 11,000 |
| With injury | 2,500 | 6,600 | 9,000 |
| No injury | 600 | 1,100 | 2,000 |
| *Drunk-driving* | 13,400 | 27,000 | 41,000 |
| With non-fatal injury | 11,300 | 24,600 | 36,000 |
| No injury | 2,400 | 2,500 | 5,000 |
| *Arson* | 2,700 | 2,400 | 5,000 |
| With non-fatal injury | 750 | 2,400 | 3,000 |
| No injury | 1,900 | 65 | 2,000 |
| *Larceny or attempt* | 9,000 | 0 | 9,000 |
| *Burglary or attempt* | 7,000 | 1,800 | 9,000 |
| *Motor vehicle theft or attempt* | 6,300 | 500 | 7,000 |
| *Total* | 105,000 | 345,000 | 450,000 |

Source: Miller, Cohen, and Wiersema (1996: Table 4).

Note: Totals were computed before rounding. "No-injury" cases involve no physical injury, but may involve psychological injury. NCVS fatal crimes = all crime deaths except drunk-driving and arson. Personal fraud/attempt is excluded to prevent possible double counting with larceny.

include them with the underlying crime would result in double-counting. According to these figures, in 1993, the cost of crime to victims totaled $450 billion. This amounts to nearly $1,800 per year for every man, woman, and child in the U.S. The largest single category is adult rape and sexual abuse, estimated to cost $127 billion. Fatal crimes and assaults are tied for second with $93 billion each. Child abuse is next, with an estimated cost of $56 billion, followed by non-fatal drunk-driving at $41 billion. Note that if the fatal drunk-driving accidents were included in the latter category, they would total $61 billion.

---

### Have crime costs increased or decreased over time?

The cost-of-crime estimates in Tables 3.1 through 3.3 are shown in 1993 dollars. That is the basis for the Miller, Cohen, and Wiersema (1996) study. To convert these figures to current dollars is not a straightforward task. As discussed in detail in the remainder of this chapter, cost-of-crime estimates are based on various types of cost—including wage losses, medical costs, the monetary value of pain, suffering, and reduced quality of life, and the statistical value of life. All of these figures change at differing rates over the years. For example, between 1993 and 2003, medical costs have increased by approximately 47 percent, while wages have increased by 37 percent. However, the cost of other goods and services has only increased by about 26 percent during this time period.

If the severity of the typical crime has changed over the years, these figures would need to be altered further. For example, if more assaults end up with gunshot wounds than they did in 1993, the current cost of an assault may be higher. Similarly, if automobiles have become safer through the use of more airbags and antilock brakes during this time period, the average harm caused by a drunk-driving accident may be less than it was in 1993. Finally, the aggregate figures in Table 3.3 assume 1993 crime levels. Crime has been steadily decreasing over the past few years, so that the aggregate burden of crime should go down accordingly.

With these caveats in mind, I have made a few simplifying assumptions and attempted to update the cost per victimization and the aggregate cost of crime. Where available, I have updated the crime victimization numbers to the latest figures (usually 2002). I have also increased the cost per crime based on the cost increases above accounting for health care costs differently from wage losses and from other tangible costs ("intangible" costs were increased at the same rate as other tangible costs, 26 percent). However, I have not changed the average "severity" of each crime type. The result is that the aggregate costs of crime in the U.S. have increased from $450 billion in 1993 to $460 billion in 2003. This is only a 2 percent increase over a 10-year period—far less than the inflation rate over that time period. This is indicative of the declining crime rate over the past decade. For example, while there were approximately 24,000 murders in 1993, this figure was reduced to 14,000 in 2003.

What does this mean for the relative burden imposed by crime? It appears that over the past decade, criminal victimization costs have decreased substantially in "real" terms. One way to see this is to compare the aggregate dollar cost to victims to total "personal income" in the United States. Thus, in 1993, total personal income was about $5.5 trillion (Council of Economic Advisors, 2004). The cost of criminal victimization ($450 billion) would represent about 8 percent of personal income. However, in 2003, total personal income in the U.S. was about $9.2 trillion. The cost of criminal victimization ($460 billion) therefore currently represents only about 5 percent of personal income. Thus, at first glance, it appears that there has been a significant reduction in the "burden" imposed by crime in the U.S.

Note that this comparison does not mean we spend 5–8 percent of our personal income on "criminal victimization." The criminal victimization figure includes intangible losses such as pain, suffering, and lost quality of life. If we were to only compare "tangible" costs of crime (about $105 billion) to personal income, criminal victimization cost about 2 percent of personal income in 1993 and 1 percent in 2003.

Of course, the above comparison excludes the cost of the criminal justice system itself—and part of the reason that crime has declined over these years is presumably owing to increases in the number of police on the street, the incapacitative effect of longer prison sentences, and other measures taken to reduce crime in the U.S. Adding the cost of the criminal justice system (about $97 billion in 1993 compared to approximately $175 billion in 2003),[1] the combined costs of crime would be $547 billion in 1993 versus $635 billion in 2003. These figures represent about 10 percent of personal income in 1993 compared to 7 percent in 2003—still a significant reduction. However, still excluded from a full accounting and comparison would be the costs of "prevention and avoidance." It is quite possible that society has increased its expenditures in this arena such that the total burden of crime has not been reduced at all.

The remainder of this chapter enumerates the cost of crime to victims that go into the tables we have just discussed. Remember that I have excluded most "third-party" and "social" costs from this chapter, and will return to them in chapter 4.

## Tangible victim costs

Victims of crime potentially suffer many losses including medical or mental health bills, lost wages and damaged or stolen property. Some violent acts result in virtually no losses or harm to victims, while others impose large costs that have a devastating impact on the financial status of victims. One victim of assault, for example, might have been punched by the offender, with little or no medical costs or lost wages. Another assault victim, however, might have spent weeks in the hospital, lost his job, and suffered hundreds of thousands of dollars in losses. Researchers and policy analysts, however, are often concerned with estimating the "typical" or "average" cost of victimization. Keep in mind that these average costs are valid for general studies and policy recommendations that relate to typical victims. However, it is sometimes important to go beyond the typical victim and analyze the average cost for a specific type of victim (elderly, child, etc.). In other cases, a particular victim's losses are most relevant. For example, if the victim is suing an offender in a personal injury lawsuit, the only relevant loss is that suffered by the victim. For now, we will focus on the "typical" victim. We will return to victim-specific losses later.

## Productivity losses

When a victim is unable to go to work or school, or perform household duties, there is a loss to both the individual victim and often to society as a whole. Reasons for such losses include not only serious injuries that require hospitalization or bed rest, but also the more mundane task of dealing with the criminal justice system. The National Crime Victim Survey (NCVS) is a national survey of a random sample of the U.S. population over the age of 12. The NCVS asks a series of questions to identify respondents who were recently victimized and to ascertain details of their victimization experience. While the NCVS asks victims to estimate the number of workdays they missed as a result of either medical care or spending time with the criminal justice system, it does not ask about days of school missed or household duties that the victim can no longer perform. While this estimate of lost workdays is a "direct" method of estimation, since the NCVS does not ask for actual wage information, one must rely upon indirect methods to determine lost wages. For example, many studies rely upon average wage rates in the U.S. population (sometimes distinguishing wages by the age and/or sex of the victim) and apply those wage rates to the reported NCVS number of hours of lost work.

Even for the lost workdays that it does survey, however, the NCVS survey underestimates losses since it only covers a six-month time period. Thus serious injuries resulting in long-term workplace disabilities are not included. Further, since many criminal trials are delayed well beyond this time frame, a victim might lose time from work appearing in court without it being captured by the NCVS. Because of the limitations of the NCVS, several studies have attempted to make more complete estimates of workday losses as well as estimate school and housework losses. These studies are briefly described below.

## Workdays

According to NCVS data, only a small percentage of victims of crime actually report that they lose time at work. Cohen, Miller, and Rossman (1993: 107) report that only 4 percent of assault victims, 7 percent of robbery victims, and 11 percent of rape victims report lost workdays. However, for those who do miss time at work, the loss can be significant: 16 days on average for rape victims, 14 days for assault victims, and 12.5 days for robbery victims. Thus, while Cohen, Miller, and Rossman (1993) estimated the average cost per victim to be quite low—about $135 for the average rape in 1987 dollars—the average loss to rape victims who did lose time at work was estimated to be almost 10 times as high—about $1,250 in 1987 dollars. Even these survey-based results rely somewhat on indirect methods, since the NCVS does not obtain wage rate information. Thus Cohen, Miller, and Rossman (1993) assumed wage rates based on the average in the population. However, it is not necessarily the case that the "typical" crime victim has average earnings. In fact, the victimization rate is significantly higher for lower-income individuals than upper-income individuals. For example, while there were reportedly 45.5 victims of violent crimes per 1,000 in the population of households with income under $7,500, and 31.2 per 1,000 in households between $7,500 and $14,999, the victimization rate was only 19.0 per 1,000 for households with income of $75,000 or more (Bureau of Justice Statistics (BJS), 2004b: Table 14). Interestingly, these ratios change considerably for property crimes, where the highest victimization rate (143 per 1,000) is for households of $75,000 or more, while households with less than $7,500 in annual income experience only a slightly smaller rate of 134 per 1,000 (BJS, 2004b: Table 15).

Since the NCVS only covers a six-month period, Miller, Cohen, and Wiersema (1996) increased the NCVS work-loss figures by estimating long-term lost workdays for those victims who were seriously injured. These long-term work-loss estimates are based on similar injuries in the workplace. Thus, for example, they estimate the average rape or sexual assault victim (including attempted rape and child abuse) loses about $2,200 in productivity (1993 dollars). Even these estimates are likely to be too small, however, since they are based on a combination of the NCVS reported short-term wage loss and long-term losses owing to similar physical injuries. However, the long-term implication of victimization may be hidden and underestimated. For example, Macmillan (2000) finds that educational attainment and lifetime earnings are lower for victims of childhood physical or sexual assault. This is partly explained by the psychological trauma that reduces self-esteem and causes depression and anxiety, leading to reduced educational attainment and ultimately lower earnings. This might be particularly true for victims who are already at the lower end of the socioeconomic scale, since they do not have the resources—either financially or socially—to overcome the trauma of victimization. Macmillan (2000) estimates the present value of reduced lifetime earnings for victims of physical or sexual assault to be $36,726. Estimated separately, the losses were $16,045 for sexual assault, $24,603 for assaults with a weapon, and $40,921 for assaults resulting in the victim being beaten. These costs are in addition to any losses estimated by previous authors.

When someone is murdered, all of their future earnings and workplace productivity are lost. Economists have long studied the present value of future earnings losses for regulatory cost–benefit analysis as well as for purposes of estimating damages in wrongful death litigation. Based on the average age of murder victims, and an assumption that murder victim earnings are average in the population, Miller, Cohen, and Wiersema (1996) estimated the present value of future wage losses to be $1 million for most murder victims. They estimated a slightly higher figure ($1.15 million) for victims of drunk-driving accidents (who tend to be younger and hence have longer expected work lives). On the other hand, arson victims—who tend to be older—were estimated to have future productivity losses of only $724,000. All of these figures include lost household services, a category we turn to next.

### Household services

Services performed in the home have value to the individual and to the rest of the family. When someone is injured, they might be unable to perform some or all of their normal household chores such as cleaning, cooking, lawn care, and home maintenance. These services need to be replaced either by another family member or by hiring outside domestic help, or they will simply go undone. In some cases, the individual who is injured will be able to perform the services, but at a slower pace. This additional time spent doing chores is also a loss, since that time could have been spent on more productive or leisurely activities.

There are no survey data available that directly assess the extent to which victims are unable to perform household services. Instead, the only estimates that have been made in this area are based on rather simplistic assumptions about the relationship between household services and workdays. Thus Miller, Cohen, and Wiersema (1996) assumed that individuals who reported in the NCVS that they lost workdays were also unable to do housework. Since there are seven days in a week and five in a normal work week, each day of work lost was assumed to translate into 7/5 days of housework. However, since some victims are not in the labor force at all, this method would undercount the number of victims who do lose household services. Thus, for those who were not employed, they assumed that their lost household service days would equal that of the lost workdays of those who are employed. The bottom line is that these assumptions more than double the number of estimated hours of time lost owing to victimization. Translating those harms into dollars, however, is even more difficult.

Economists have long recognized that household services are valuable even if not compensated for in normal labor markets. However, placing a dollar value on those services is both conceptually and empirically a challenge. Economic theory would tell us that if individuals are rational and utility maximizing, and if workers are free to come and go in the labor market, then we could infer the value of household services by the "opportunity cost" of the individual's time. Opportunity cost is an economic concept that places the value of a particular good or service at its cost in the next best alternative. For example, if a woman decides to stay home with her young children instead of working, we can value her time at home as being equal to the wages she would have earned in the workforce. By giving up wages, the opportunity cost of her time is her forgone earnings. But what if this woman spends 50 hours per week on household services? Do we assume that she could have worked overtime and value the additional 10 hours per week at overtime wages? That would only make sense if she did have that opportunity of working overtime. What if the woman has never worked? Do we assume she could have earned the same as an average woman in the workplace? Or do we attempt to project her earning capacity based on her intellectual ability and educational attainment? For purposes of estimating average losses in a population, we can probably ignore the latter problem by simply assuming the average in the population (perhaps based on age and educational attainment).

However, there is a more serious conceptual problem with using "opportunity cost" as a measure of lost household services. Suppose two different women—a doctor and a waitress—leave the workforce to raise a family. If they are both injured and temporarily unable to do housework, is their loss the same? Not if the "opportunity cost" approach is used. In fact, we might value the former doctor's loss at many times that of the waitress. Yet those services could be replaced at the same cost. Thus another method of valuing lost household services is to estimate the cost of replacing those services on the open market. This "replacement cost" approach is not without its own problems. For example, it ignores the "joint production" nature of many activities such as child rearing and gardening. While a mother might watch her children playing in the backyard while she is gardening, it is unlikely that she would be able to replace those services by hiring either a gardener who would watch the children or a babysitter who would agree to do the gardening. In addition, although these activities could be replaced by hiring a nanny and a gardener respectively, neither one properly compensates for the loss. In the case of child rearing, no nanny can replace the loving care of a mother, so that the true loss to the individual is higher than the cost of replacing the services. In the case of the gardener, if the housewife enjoys the activity and obtains "leisure" out of gardening, then replacing her services by hiring a gardener would be an overestimate of the value of those services.

The few studies to date that have incorporated household service losses in the cost of victimization have used the "replacement cost" approach to valuing those services. Based on the mix of services normally provided by men and women in the household, Douglass, Kenney, and Miller (1990) estimated an average wage rate of $5.65 per hour in 1987 dollars for women (about $9.87 per hour in 2004), and $6.34 per hour for men (about $11.07 per hour in 2000). These wage rates exclude fringe benefits, which would generally be 20–30 percent of income. The higher wage rate for men reflects their tendency to perform tasks that would be more expensive to replace (e.g. working on cars, and mechanical, electrical, and plumbing work in the home). These figures were used by Miller, Cohen, and Wiersema (1996) in estimating the value of lost household services to victims of crime. As indicated above, for victims of crime who also lost workdays or who were not employed but received similar injuries as those who lost workdays, they assumed the number of household service days lost were equal to 7/5 of the workdays lost. For murdered victims, however, they relied upon the Douglass, Kenney, and Miller (1990) study that estimated the average annual value of household production by age, sex, and workplace status. For example, while a 40 to 44-year-old woman who is currently employed is estimated to provide $8,323 in annual household services (1987 dollars), that figure increases to $13,534 if she is not employed. Males of the same age are estimated to provide $4,094 in household services if employed, and $6,866 in services if not employed.

### School days

Although the NCVS does not report lost school days owing to victim injury, it does record employment status and whether or not the victim is a full-time student. The few studies to date that have attempted to estimate the number of school days lost have arbitrarily assumed that students would be out of school to the same extent that adults with similar victim-related injuries reportedly are out of work. This may or may not be a good approximation for the actual number of school days missed.

Conceptually, placing a dollar value on a lost school day is even more difficult than it is for household services. Presumably, someone who misses one day in school can make up the work they missed by working a few extra hours after school. The opportunity cost of their additional time learning might be considered a loss in that case. Of course, for most students, it is not clear what the opportunity cost of their time is worth—if anything. A high-school or college student might otherwise work and earn money. Younger students might also give up the value of their time doing household chores—although this would only apply to the families lucky enough to have children who actually do their allotted chores! Even then, there is no obvious method for estimating the opportunity cost of their time when they are spending the time watching television or playing video games, for example. Alternatively, if enough school is lost that an entire grade must be repeated, or there is some permanent reduction in earning capacity, this could be translated directly into reduced earnings. However, that is only likely to be the case in very severe cases.

The few studies that have estimated a value of lost school days have assumed that the value per day is equal to the cost of providing education for that child. For example, the value of each lost school year could be esti-mated at $7,284, based upon the annual cost per pupil.[2] Based on an average school year of approximately 165 days, this translates into about $44 per school day. In some ways this is conceptually an attractive measure for the social cost of a lost school day, since society obviously believes it is worth spending at least that much on education. In fact, since there are posi-tive private and social returns to schooling, using the cost of a school day as a proxy for its value is actually an underestimate. For example, Haveman and Wolfe (1984) catalogued all of the potential private and public benefits associated with education and reviewed the empirical literature and state of the art in estimation techniques. They concluded that the total non-market benefits of education approximately equal the market benefits. Thus it is possible that the estimated value of school days lost would need to be doubled. Ultimately, however, except in extreme cases where lost time at school cannot be made up, the true marginal cost of lost school days is more appropriately measured as the marginal opportunity cost of the pupil's time than as the average cost of education to the government. As discussed above, unless one wants to place a positive value on playing video games, the mar-ginal opportunity cost of a pupil's time is probably quite low in most cases!

This rather mechanical approach to valuing the educational loss owing to victimization is outweighed by more recent attempts to estimate the long-term reduction in educational attainment, socioeconomic status and lifetime earnings. As noted above, Macmillan (2000) recently made the first esti-mates of these long-term effects, with an average of $36,726 in present-value terms for victims of violence. These figures dwarf the value of lost school days estimated by previous authors.

## Medical costs

As discussed earlier, the Bureau of Justice Statistics sponsors an ongoing survey of criminal victimizations, the National Crime Victimization Survey (NCVS). However, the NCVS significantly underestimates actual medical costs. Although respondents are asked if they received medical treatment as a result of a recent victimization, the reference period for the NCVS is crimes committed during the previous six months. Since a crime will have occurred an average of about three months prior to its being reported to the NCVS, any medical costs are necessarily limited to those short-term costs. Even short-term costs are likely to be underestimated, however, since hospi-tal bills are often sent directly to insurance companies, and may arrive months after hospitalization.

Because the direct method of estimation is known to exclude significant costs, recent attempts to estimate the medical costs to crime victims have relied upon indirect methods. Miller, Cohen, and Wiersema (1996) obtained all available data on each crime victim in the NCVS (e.g. type of injury, whether or not hospitalized, and age and sex of victim), and combined that information with cost of injury data from hospitalization charges reported in several states that provide information on the cause of injury (including "intentional injury"). Thus, for example, the medical costs incurred by an assault victim with a broken bone is estimated from hospital data on the cost of broken bones to intentional injury victims. This procedure resulted in estimates of tangible costs that are considerably higher than those of the NCVS.

Medical costs for some categories of crime are even more difficult to obtain. No estimates appear to be available for the medical care costs of murder victims, since the NCVS is only based on living household members. Thus, as a first approximation, previous research on medical costs associated with murder has used the medical care costs of workers' compensation cases resulting in fatality. Whether typical murder victims experience higher or lower medical care fees than worker-related fatalities is unknown.

The NCVS also restricts its analysis to members of a household age 12 or older. Thus, to the extent that children under age 12 are victimized, the NCVS underestimates this component of crime costs. Miller, Cohen, and Wiersema (1996) estimated the medical costs for child abuse victims by assuming that the distribution of injuries is similar to adult assault cases (e.g. similar percentages have broken arms) and by estimating actual medical costs from hospitalization records in child abuse cases. These estimates are admittedly very crude. We simply do not have good estimates of the costs of child abuse.

## Mental health care costs

Mental health care costs are among the least studied costs of crime. Although there are many clinical studies documenting the importance of mental health care for crime victims, the NCVS does not ask respondents about their mental health care following victimization. Post-traumatic stress disorder (PTSD) is now well established as a clinical diagnosis often caused by criminal victimization. Among the symptoms are "compulsive repetition" of the traumatic event in the victim's mind, as well as "numbness or unresponsiveness to, or reduced involvement with, the external world" (Horowitz, 1986: 244). The cause of PTSD is usually an event that "lies outside the range of common experiences . . . (such as) . . . rapes, muggings, assaults, military combat, torture, natural disasters, traumatically frightening or painful medical experiences, deaths of loved ones, and accidents such as airplane and car crashes" (p. 244). Wirtz and Harrell (1987) report that high levels of fear, anxiety, and stress persist in crime victims six months after their victimization. They found that physical assault victims (rape, domestic violence, and non-domestic assault) had higher levels of fear, anxiety, and stress than nonassault victims (robbery and burglary). A nationally representative survey of women (Kilpatrick, Edmunds, and Seymour, 1992) estimated that 31 percent of rape victims (compared to 5 percent in the non-victim sample) ever had PTSD. Major depression was reported by 30 percent of rape victims, compared to 10 percent of the non-victim sample. This was one of the first studies to document the extent of mental illness in a nationally representative victim population.[3]

Cohen and Miller (1998) conducted a stratified random sample of 168 mental health care professionals, including social workers, pastoral counselors, psychologists, and psychiatrists. Respondents were asked to identify the total number of clients they treated and the percentage of those who were treated primarily as a result of victimization. Other questions included in the survey were the number of visits for a typical victim and the cost per visit. This information was collected for each type of crime. While the Cohen and Miller (1998) study is somewhat limited in that it asked mental health care providers over the phone for an estimate of their patient load (and did not involve detailed analysis of patient records), the results of this survey are illuminating. The vast majority (80 percent) of surveyed mental health professionals who were actively engaged in a clinical practice reportedly treated at least one patient during the prior year who was being treated primarily as a result of criminal victimization. Overall, 30 percent of the average client population of active mental health care professionals consisted of crime victims, while the median percentage was 20 percent.

As shown in Table 3.4 (overleaf), mental health care for victims of crime can be substantial. An estimated 25–50 percent of all rape victims receive mental health counseling, with the average cost to those who receive treatment being over $1,700 (1991 dollars). This figure excludes any crisis counseling at rape crisis centers or emergency rooms immediately following a rape. In contrast, victims of robbery or household burglary only rarely seek mental health counseling as a result of their victimization, with rates estimated to be less than half of 1 percent for burglary victims and between 2 and 6 percent for victims of robbery.

However, it is important to note that mental health care is as much dependent on ability to pay and insurance coverage as it is with the need for care precipitated by victimization. Thus mental health care costs vastly understate the impact of victimization on the mental health and quality of life of victims. We will return to other methods of measuring quality of life in the next section when we discuss the intangible costs of crime.

## Property losses

Despite being among the most tangible and easily identified losses, stolen and damaged property is one of the most insignificant costs of most crimes. For example, Miller, Cohen, and Wiersema (1996) estimate the average rape victim has about $100 in property losses compared to $500 in medical

*Table 3.4* Mental health care costs for victims of crime (1991 dollars)

| Crime | Cost per victim treated ($) | % of victims receiving treatment |
| --- | --- | --- |
| Recent child sexual abuse | 1,160 | 25–49 |
| Recent child physical abuse | 1,798 | 34–15 |
| Child sexual abuse years earlier | 2,446 | 7–15 |
| Physical child abuse years earlier | 2,178 | 3–5 |
| Attempted or completed rape | 1,771 | 25–49 |
| Assault including domestic violence | 2,015 | 4 |
| Robbery | 1,371 | 2–6 |
| Burglary or theft | 1,317 | 0.3 |
| Witnessing a murder or losing a loved one to murder | 2,330 | 150–250* |
| Drunk-driving victims | 1,309 | 2–4 |

Source: Cohen and Miller (1998).

* On average, it is estimated that for every murder victim there are 1.5 to 2.5 people (most likely relatives) who receive mental health care treatment.

expenses and $2,200 in mental health care costs. Even robbery victims who suffer an average property value loss of $750 bear productivity and wage losses of $950 on average. The largest property loss crimes are motor vehicle theft, drunk-driving accidents, and arson, all of which involve expensive tangible property. In the aggregate, however, property losses are still a significant portion of the tangible costs of crime. Based on the data in Miller, Cohen, and Wiersema (1996), about 24 percent of all tangible costs of crime are property losses. This is primarily because of the larger volume of property crimes as opposed to the smaller number of more serious violent crimes resulting in medical costs and lost wages. For example, the NCVS estimates there are more than three times as many property crimes as personal crimes—17.5 million property crimes versus 5.5 million crimes against the person in 2002 (BJS, 2003a).

### Indirect costs of victimization

Following victimization, individuals might alter their everyday behavior. The indirect consequences of victimization can be far-reaching and beyond the scope of any empirical study to date. According to Burt and Katz (1985: 330), "During the weeks or months following the [rape], women frequently make costly changes in their lifestyles; this may involve moving to a 'better' neighborhood, buying expensive security systems, or avoiding work situations which they suddenly perceive as dangerous." In Chapter 4 we will examine the extent to which potential victims take similar precautions in order to reduce their personal risk of becoming a crime victim. The only study I am aware of to date to empirically estimate some of these indirect effects on crime victims is Dugan (1999), who estimates the likelihood that individuals will move following a criminal victimization. Dugan estimates a baseline rate of 4.5 percent of households who move (if there is no victimization), compared to 5.6 percent for those who were victimized by property crime in the previous year. Interestingly, Dugan found that victims of violent crime were no more likely to move than victims of property crime. Finally, Dugan also found there is often a lag between victimization and moving, which suggests that crime victims might live with increased fear, increase their precautionary expenditures (e.g. purchase burglar alarms), or otherwise incur costs prior to moving.

## Intangible victim costs

As discussed in Chapter 2, economists have employed various methods to estimate intangible costs. Some of these approaches are based on the *ex ante* costs to society as a whole—potential victims. Those methods and cost estimates will be discussed in Chapter 4. In this chapter we focus on victim costs (as opposed to community or potential victim costs). Thus the approaches we focus on here are *ex post* measures, based on the costs actually borne by crime victims.

### *Pain, suffering, and reduced quality of life*

The intangible victim costs of pain, suffering, and reduced quality of life are the most difficult to measure and subject to considerable uncertainty and controversy. Yet, when measured, they are inevitably the largest component of victim costs. Until recently, the only attempts to value these intangible victim losses have used the method I developed in 1988, based on a combination of jury awards and the risk of death. Jury awards are used to value pain and suffering for non-fatal injuries, while estimates of the statistical "value of life" are multiplied by the risk of death for each type of crime to arrive at the "risk of death" component of costs. The most recent estimates, published in 1996, are reproduced in the column titled "Quality of life" in Table 3.1. Note that there are no quality-of-life estimates for larceny, since these crimes by definition involve no human contact and hence no risk of injury or death. Even burglary is estimated to have an intangible cost of $300 per offense, however, based on the fact that a small fraction of burglaries involve incidents where someone is home at the time—and some of these incidents eventually result in a homicide. The ratio of intangible to tangible costs varies considerably by crime, with burglary being on the low end— intangibles being about a third of tangibles—and rape being at the high end—intangibles being 15 times greater than tangible losses.

One limitation of the approach used in Miller, Cohen, and Wiersema (1996) as well as my earlier estimates of the cost of crime is that the intangible costs of property crimes such as burglary are based on the probability of being a homicide victim. This is likely to underestimate the fear and feeling of being 'violated' that accompanies being a burglary victim. As discussed further in Chapter 4, estimates that look at the *ex ante* willingness to pay to reduce property crimes such as burglary suggest that potential victims do place a relatively high value on these crimes.

### Lost quality of life for fatal crimes

The approach that Cohen (1988a) and Miller, Cohen, and Wiersema (1996) used to value the lost quality of life for fatal crimes is based on *ex ante* willingness to pay to reduce the risk of death. As discussed in Chapter 2, most of these estimates are made in the context of worker wage-rate differentials for riskier jobs or consumer purchases of risk-reducing products. They are not

---

#### Cost-of-crime estimates outside the U.S.

Cost-of-crime estimates are not within the sole purview of U.S. researchers. Indeed, governments and academics around the world have begun to prepare estimates of the monetary cost of crime. However, the methodologies used by these various researchers vary considerably. Few of them take into account the largest cost of crime— intangible pain, suffering, and lost quality of life. One exception is in the U.K., where economists at the Home Office developed estimates of both tangible and intangible costs of crime (Brand and Price, 2001). Their approach to estimating the intangible costs of pain, suffering, and lost quality of life relied upon the "direct" contingent valuation survey method discussed in Chapter 2. However, they did not have available to them any surveys of the public on their willingness to pay for reduced criminal victimization. Instead, they relied upon earlier studies of injuries to automobile crash victims. Thus they inferred the cost of an assault from perceived seriousness and the most similar automobile accident injury they could find. Their approach is thus virtually identical to that used in Cohen (1988a), except that they use willingness-to-pay estimates instead of jury awards to value lost quality of life. For example, Brand and Price (2001: Table 4.1) show the average cost of a "serious wounding" to be £14,000 in lost productivity, £8,506 in health service costs, and £97,000 in "emotional and physical impact on victims." In this example, pain and suffering is about four times the out-of-pocket costs of lost wages and medical costs. This is very similar to the ratios that are found in Miller, Cohen, and Wiersema, shown here in Table 3.1. For example, the out-of-pocket costs for NCVS assault with injury in Table 3.1 is $4,800, compared to $19,300 in lost quality of life. This is also about a four-to-one ratio.

Other countries are also beginning to produce cost-of-crime esti-mates. However, few of these estimates include a monetary value of intangible losses such as pain, suffering, and reduced quality of life. When estimates are made, they are oftentimes based on U.S. or U.K. estimates of intangible losses which do not necessarily translate properly into the other country's culture. Currently, I am aware of published studies in English in Australia (Mayhew, 2003), Canada (Brantingham and Easton, 1998), France (Palle and Godefroy, 2000), as well as non-English studies completed in Colombia and the Nether-lands. However, there is growing interest around the world in prepar-ing cost-of-crime estimates. For example, a conference in March 2004 funded by the Finnish National Council for Crime Prevention in co-operation with the European Forum for Urban Safety and the Swedish Council for Crime Prevention brought together researchers from Euro-pean countries to compare methods and cost estimates. This is the first such international conference on the "cost of crime," and the outcome will no doubt lead to a growing cadre of researchers around the world interested in this topic.

Average cost of crime to victims in the U.K. (1999 pounds sterling)

| | Property stolen or damaged (£) | Lost output (£) | Health services and victim services (£) | Subtotal: tangible costs (£) | Emotional and physi-cal impact on victims (£) | Total cost (£) |
|---|---|---|---|---|---|---|
| Homicide | – | 370,000 | 5,330 | 382,330 | 700,000 | 1.1m |
| Serious wounding | – | 14,000 | 8,506 | 22,500 | 97,000 | 119,500 |
| Other wounding | – | 400 | 206 | 600 | 120 | 720 |
| Common assault | – | 20 | 6 | 26 | 240 | 266 |
| Sexual offenses | – | 2,000 | 1,220 | 3,220 | 12,000 | 15,220 |
| Robbery/mugging | 310 | 420 | 196 | 926 | 2,400 | 3,326 |
| Burglary in dwelling | 830 | 40 | 4 | 874 | 550 | 1,424 |
| Theft (not vehicle) | 130 | 4 | 0 | 134 | 100 | 234 |
| Vehicle theft | 500 | 20 | 0 | 520 | 220 | 740 |
| Criminal damage | 190 | 30 | 0 | 220 | 200 | 420 |

Source: Brand and Price (2001).

taken directly from studies of the willingness to pay for reductions in the risk of fatal crimes. The value of a "statistical life" that is implied by these studies includes future wages and productivity as well as lost quality of life. Miller (1989) proposed a method of breaking these estimates into their component parts. Miller, Cohen, and Wiersema (1996) adopted this method and updated the figures to 1993 dollars, where $2.7 million was taken to be the statistical value of life for a 38-year-old male, and $1.9 million was estimated to be the "lost quality of life" component. This figure was adjusted to the average age of the typical crime victim. Since these estimates were made, more recent estimates place the statistical value of a life for the average worker in the U.S. between $3 and $9 million (Viscusi, 2000). Thus the cost of fatal crimes could be as much as three times the amount shown in Table 3.1.

## Police and fire emergency services

One of the most immediate costs of victimization is often the emergency personnel dispatched to assist the victim. Police and fire department resources are often dispatched to the scene of the crime to ensure that the victim is properly cared for and that further damage (in the case of arson) is not done. According to Miller, Cohen, and Wiersema (1996), dispatching emergency vehicles costs on average about $200 per incident for most crimes. The emergency responses to arson and murder are higher, about $1,000 to $2,000. These costs are shown in Table 3.1. Note that not all victims require such an emergency response, however. Thus, while an average response cost might be $200, the average cost per assault is much less—about $26 per incident. This is because many assaults are not reported to police, and those that are reported might not be severe enough to warrant emergency services. On the other hand, most cases of fatal crime and arson involve some emergency services.

The cost of emergency response is only a small portion of the total cost of police and fire department expenditures related to crime. In particular, police and fire investigations designed to capture offenders and deter future offenders are more properly studied as part of "society's response to victimization" in Chapter 4.

## Victim services

Victim service organizations provide many services to victims of crime including counseling, temporary shelter, and financial assistance. This section focuses on another cost of victimization—the cost of victim assistance programs designed to help counsel and otherwise ease the trauma associated with victimization. In the following section, we will examine financial assistance to victims as a means of shifting some of the financial burden of the cost of crime away from the victim. In some ways these costs might be more properly labeled "society's response to victimization" rather than a direct cost imposed by the victimization itself. Hence they might reasonably be included in Chapter 4 instead of this chapter. However, in the absence of these victim assistance programs, victims would presumably suffer even further in pain, suffering, and lost quality of life. Thus these costs are just one method of reducing some of the other costs imposed on victims. In some cases, they really are preventative—as in battered women's shelters that might reduce the chance of a reoccurrence of the victimization.

The National Organization for Victim Assistance (NOVA), one of the first non-profit organizations established as a national clearinghouse for victims' rights, maintains a listing of over 6,000 victim assistance programs around the country (http://www.try-nova.org/mission.html). Another non-profit organization, the National Center for Victims of Crime, claims it is affiliated with over 10,000 grass roots organizations around the country (http://www.ncvc.org/main/main.htm). Although I do not know how much is spent on victim services by state or local governments or private organizations, there are several ways of arriving at "ballpark" estimates of expenditures. According to the Office for Victims of Crime (2000), more than 3,000 programs were supported with federal matching funds during 1998, with total federal assistance being $275 million that year. The Victims of Crime Act (VOCA) authorizing these grants requires at least a 25 percent match for existing programs, although this may be a "soft" match (e.g. 'in-kind' donations, such as volunteer time). Thus, at the very least, $366 million was spent that year in federally assisted programs. However, Cohen, Miller, and Rossman (1993: 102) estimated that VOCA funds could account for as little as 18 percent (or less) of expenditures on victim assistance programs. That level of funding would imply that $1.5 billion or more is spent on victim assistance programs. If that is the case, it would be a significant increase from the $200 million estimated to have been spent in 1986. These figures also underestimate, to the extent that they exclude the value of volunteer time spent on outreach activities for crime victims.

Most victim assistance programs focus on violent crimes—often sexual assaults, child abuse, and domestic violence. It is difficult to allocate the funding across crimes, since many programs serve more than one type of crime victim and no ongoing data collection program exists to determine where these funds are used. Cohen, Miller, and Rossman (1993: 103) estimated that about 23 percent of these funds are used to assist rape victims, 33 percent for spouse abuse, 19 percent for child abuse, and the remaining 25 percent for other crimes or victims in general. Table 3.1 includes these cost estimates. However, they are estimated to be a very small percentage of the overall cost of crime to victims.

## Victim compensation and tort awards

Although victims of crime might suffer many or all of the losses discussed in this chapter, in some instances they are reimbursed for their monetary losses. Public assistance programs such as Medicaid or unemployment compensation or other forms of private insurance might pay for medical costs or lost wages. In other instances, a court might require an offender to pay restitution to the victim—generally for damaged or stolen property. However, since not all victimizations result in a convicted offender, and many offenders have little if any assets or legitimate jobs, restitution awards will never compensate all victims for their monetary losses. As a result, victim compensation funds have been established in all 50 states to provide some financial support and assistance to victims in need. Finally, in some cases, victims might pursue private remedies through civil tort awards. However, because many violent offenders are judgment-proof, this remedy has limited applicability. Indeed, oftentimes tort awards in cases of violent crime are made against third parties—not the offenders.

## Restitution

Restitution is a court-ordered payment from the offender to the victim and is designed to compensate (at least partially) the victim for his or her monetary losses.[4] Restitution is most likely to be ordered in cases of property crimes where the loss to the victim is money or property. However, restitution may also be ordered by the court to reimburse victims of violent crime for medical costs and lost wages—both past and future. In some cases, restitution might even be ordered to help support the survivors of homicide victims. Although restitution dates back to biblical times, it was seldom used in the U.S. until recently. U.S. law did not adopt the English method of criminal prosecution whereby the victim brought charges against the offender. Instead, since crimes in the U.S. are prosecuted by the government, victims (until recently) had few rights or remedies in the formal criminal process. It was not until the 1930s that a few states began to adopt laws that permitted restitution—often as part of suspended sentences and probation (Frank, 1992: 111). By the mid-1970s, the federal government had begun to encourage states to adopt restitution programs by providing funding. Several laws enacted between 1982 and 1994 at the federal level mandated full restitution in federal-level criminal cases.[5] Of course, since most criminal cases are brought at the state and local level, these laws have only a small impact on victims of violent crime. During this time, however, every state passed some type of mandatory restitution. As of 1996, 29 states had followed federal law in mandating restitution in all cases, unless the presiding judge offers compelling reasons not to do so. Others require restitution only in cases involving violent crime, while others mandate restitution only in property crime cases (National Center for Victims of Crime, 1997).

Despite these laws, there is evidence that imposition and collection of restitution is less than widespread. A recent survey of convicted felons in state court found that only 14 percent of all offenders were ordered to pay restitution (BJS, 2003b). Only 26 percent of all property offenders (e.g. burglary, larceny, motor vehicle theft, and fraud) were ordered to pay restitution. Another study found that while the average restitution order was $3,368, on average, only 54 percent of the amount ordered was paid (BJS, 1995). Given these figures, it is not surprising to learn that lack of adequate restitution is one of the most common complaints by victims. For example, a study of victims in 1980 found that 61 percent viewed monetary restitution as the fairest form of punishment, and 51 percent indicated dissatisfaction with restitution, mostly because they felt the amount imposed was insufficient (Smith, Davis, and Millenbrand, 1989).

## Victim compensation programs

In 1984 the Victims of Crime Act (VOCA) established the Crime Victims Fund in the U.S., which reimburses states for up to 40 percent of their annual compensation payments to crime victims.[6] Compensation programs provide financial assistance to victims of nearly every type of violent crime including rape, robbery, assault, sexual abuse, drunk-driving, and domestic violence. The programs pay for expenses such as medical care, mental health counseling, lost wages, and, in cases of homicide, funerals and loss of support (National Association of Crime Victim Compensation Boards, 2002). With a few exceptions, however, they do not cover lost, stolen, or damaged property. Compensation programs are "payers of last resort," meaning that the victim must exhaust all other sources of insurance or public benefits that could pay for medical care, funeral benefits, or counseling before receiving compensation.

State programs have established limits to the maximum benefits available to victims that typically range from $10,000 to $25,000, although a few states have lower or higher maximums. Nationally, the average amount paid to each victim applying for compensation is $2,000. In 1996 state compensation programs paid approximately $240 million to more than 110,000 victims nationwide (Office for Victims of Crime, 1997). However, nearly half of this amount is paid by two states with the largest programs—California and Texas. This represents less than a quarter of 1 percent of the $105 billion tangible losses shown in Table 3.3. Even if we only include medical costs, the $240 million compensation represents about 1.3 percent of the estimated $18 billion medical costs borne annually by victims of crime.

In addition to providing funding to states, VOCA established some minimum standards that state programs must adopt in order to receive federal funding, and provided the impetus for states to adopt other measures deemed to be lacking from existing programs. Nevertheless, benefits vary considerably from state to state. Not all states provide emergency assistance for immediate needs of food, shelter, and medical assistance. Some have minimum-loss requirements while others have maximum reimbursements. These dollar limits might hurt those who need the most help. Another problem with victim compensation programs is that they are not always adequately publicized so that victims are not made aware of this assistance.

Like any government program, concern over fraud and abuse has prompted officials to write rules to safeguard against those who might take advantage of the program. That is one reason why damaged—or stolen—

property claims are rarely allowed. Yet these restrictions inevitably limit the availability of funds to some otherwise deserving victims. This is especially true with violent crimes where many victims know—often intimately—the perpetrators. For example, some states do not permit payments to domestic abuse victims who are still living with their batterer. Presumably, some of that money might be stolen or used by the batterer—or the two individuals could engage in fraud to collect victim compensation awards. Another eligibility requirement is often that the victim cannot be engaged in criminal activity or in some way contribute to the crime being committed. Thus, for example, if a homicide victim was engaged in criminal activity at the time of his death, that victim's surviving spouse and children might not be eligible for benefits.

Aside from the 40 percent federal matching funds, a large portion of the funding for victim compensation programs comes from the offenders through court fees or fines. In that sense, the funds are similar to restitution, although there is no direct correspondence between the offender and the victim. Victims may receive payment irrespective of whether or not their perpetrators were caught or had paid any court fees.

## Tort awards

Although some victims are compensated through restitution or victim compensation programs, these sources seldom cover total losses. Even if all out-of-pocket costs are reimbursed, restitution and victim compensation programs rarely, if ever, compensate victims for pain, suffering, or lost quality of life. A judgment in a civil suit can provide such compensation—at least under U.S. federal and state law. The theory behind tort damages is to make the victim "whole." While this concept is not clearly defined, juries are generally instructed to award an amount that would make the victim whole in their eyes.[7] However, until recently, victims seldom filed legal tort claims for injuries sustained as a result of violent behavior. Sherman and Klein (1984) analyzed tens of thousands of civil tort cases reported on from 1958–82 by the American Trial Lawyers' Association (ATLA). They found only 186 security-related cases. It should be noted that the ATLA data set is clearly not an exhaustive list nor a representative sample of civil tort actions in the U.S. Nevertheless, given the several million annual victimizations in the U.S., it is clear that few victims sue for damages. By the early 1980s some growth had been noted, as about 30 cases per year were reported on during the 1980–2 time period. More recently, Cohen and Miller (2003) reported on 976 jury awards for offenses that could be classified as "physical assaults" and 277 cases of "sexual assault" or rape. These cases were tried between 1980 and 1991 and are taken from Jury Verdict Research (JVR) data. By 1988 they reported approximately 200 cases per year. Although JVR data are not entirely comprehensive or representative, by 1991 the company reportedly collected approximately 18,000 jury verdicts annually from around the country. This represents about 40 percent of all verdicts in the U.S.[8] If we assume that they also collect 40 percent of crime victim verdicts, then there were approximately 500 jury awards to crime victims in the U.S. per year by 1991. Furthermore, since 95 percent of lawsuits settle prior to trial, there may be as many as 10,000 lawsuits filed annually by crime victims. However, even 10,000 lawsuits represent less than half of 1 percent of all crime victimizations annually.

One reason there are so few civil lawsuits by victims is that offenders seldom have adequate assets to make such suits worthwhile. An exception has been in the case of incidents that occur on third-party premises where there is an allegation of inadequate protection afforded by the third party. These suits have often been directed at businesses such as retail establishments, hotels, parking lots, and apartment buildings (Carrington, 1978 and 1983). A second reason for the small number of lawsuits is that few attorneys were aware of the potential value of such cases. This changed considerably in the 1980s as several prominent victim advocacy groups conducted research and training for lawyers, and spearheaded an effort to provide legal advice and advocacy for crime victims.[9] High-profile cases in recent years have further heightened the legal profession and the public's awareness of this option. Perhaps the most prominent of these cases was decided in February 1997, when the families of Ronald Goldman and Nicole Brown Simpson were awarded $33.5 million after a jury found O.J. Simpson liable for their deaths. Cases like this have dramatically raised the consciousness not only of the public and the legal community about civil legal remedies for victims, but of the victim service field as well.

Aside from the difficulty in collecting damages from offenders who do not have adequate assets, there are many legal barriers making it difficult for certain crime victims to seek civil remedies. For example, victims of child abuse might not discover the relationship between their psychological injuries and the abuse until they are adults—well beyond normal statutes of limitations in which people must file lawsuits. In response, many states have passed laws extending the statute of limitations for bringing lawsuits against abusers until years after the child has reached 18.

Although civil litigation might help compensate some victims, it is not a costless remedy. According to Kakalik and Pace (1986: 68–70), legal transactions costs exceeded the total amount of compensation paid through the tort system in 1985. For every dollar in compensation awarded to the plaintiff, about $1.13 was spent on legal transactions costs. Moreover, for every dollar compensation paid, the plaintiff only kept about 70 cents after paying legal fees and expenses (even less if one includes the value of the plaintiff's time and other expenses such as transportation).

## Demographic breakdown of costs

Criminal victimization is not spread out evenly over the population. Instead, certain demographic groups are more likely to be victims than others. As shown in Table 3.5, about 31 out of every 1,000 Americans are victimized by a serious violent offense (murder, robbery, rape or sexual assault, and aggravated assault) each year. However, this rate is about 50 percent higher for young people, about 44 per 1,000 for age 12–15 and 58 per 1,000 for those age 16–19. Afterwards, victimization rates steadily decline. By age 65, the risk is nearly a tenth that of the average risk—only 3.4 out of 1,000 individuals. Note that these NCVS estimates exclude crimes against children under age 12. They also undercount some categories of violence such as domestic and child abuse and rape and sexual assaults. Miller, Cohen, and Wiersema (1996) augmented these official estimates with independent studies of domestic violence, child abuse, rape, and sexual assault. These figures have been included in Tables 3.1 through 3.4.

The cost of violence does not necessarily correspond to the risk levels identified above. For example, a serious injury that impairs the victim's ability to be gainfully employed will have a significantly higher wage loss if the victim is age 18 and has his or her entire worklife ahead, compared to a 60-year-old victim who might be approaching retirement age. The productivity loss estimates that are reported in Table 3.2 take into account the age of the victim, but not their income, since income is not reported by the NCVS.

In addition, it is not necessarily the case that the same victimization results in the same degree of injury across victim age categories. Thus, for example, a physical assault against a healthy young male might result in considerably less severe injuries than a similar incident against an elderly victim. Injured elderly victims are more likely than younger victims to suffer a serious injury following a violent victimization. According to NCVS data, while 9 percent of violent crime victims age 65 or older suffer "serious injuries," only 5 percent of younger victims suffer these same injuries. Serious injuries are defined here as broken bones, loss of teeth, internal injuries, loss of consciousness, rape or attempted rape injuries, or undetermined injuries requiring two or more days of hospitalization. In addition, when injured, nearly 50 percent of older victims receive medical care in a hospital, compared to only about 25 percent of younger victims (BJS, 1994). These differential injury severity rates are also taken into account in Tables 3.1 through 3.4.

Table 3.6 compares the rate of victimization by income. Victimization occurs most often against individuals who can least afford to bear the costs of crime—those with lower incomes. For example, while the overall rate of becoming a victim of a serious violent crime was 30.6 per 1,000 in 2002, that rate was 45.5 per 1,000 for households with income under $7,500, and 31.2 for those with incomes between $7,500 and $14,999. Those with the highest income, over $75,000 per year, have the lowest victimization rate, only 19 per 1,000. As shown in Table 3.7, victimization rates also vary by race and gender. The victimization rate for black males is about 50 percent higher than for white females. As shown in Table 3.7, a significant portion of the cost of crime to victims is borne by males between the ages of 12 and 24.

*Table 3.5* Rate of victimization (per 1,000 population) per year by crime by age

| Age of victim | All serious violent crime | Rape and sexual assault | Robbery | Aggravated assault |
|---|---|---|---|---|
| Combined | 30.6 | 1.1 | 2.2 | 4.3 |
| 12–15 | 44.4 | 2.1 | 3.0 | 5.0 |
| 16–19 | 58.2 | 5.5 | 4.0 | 11.9 |
| 20–24 | 47.4 | 2.9 | 4.7 | 10.1 |
| 25–34 | 26.3 | 0.6 | 2.8 | 5.2 |
| 35–49 | 18.2 | 0.5 | 1.5 | 3.5 |
| 50–64 | 10.7 | 0.2 | 1.6 | 1.7 |
| 65 or older | 3.4 | 0.1 | 1.0 | 0.7 |

Source: Figures based on average victimization rates in 2002 taken from U.S. Bureau of Justice Statistics (2004: Table 3, "Victimization rates for persons age 12 and over, by type of crime and age of victims").

## Economic and white-collar crimes

Economic or white-collar crimes such as fraud, theft of services, and anti-trust violations are notoriously difficult to quantify because victims often do not know they have been subject to a criminal offense. Even for those crimes where victims know their losses, there is no central government survey or reporting mechanism to tally these crimes or their costs. Government regulatory or enforcement agencies often collect these figures and may report them as they see fit. However, it is often difficult to verify their methodology and to know if figures can be compared in any meaningful way. Most estimates of the cost of economic crimes are based on either surveys of potential victims to ascertain their experiences, or collection of government data on prosecutions.

Unlike street crime, which is systematically measured through victim surveys, no comprehensive surveys of the incidence or cost of white-collar crimes exist. Although various estimates exist, the sampling methodology and crime definitions are seldom transparent, making comparability across crime particularly difficult. However, if the estimates are to be believed, white-collar crime causes tangible losses far in excess of tangible losses associated with street crimes. For example, a 2002 study by the Association of Certified Fraud Examiners reports that the average business loses about 6 percent of its total annual revenue to fraud and abuse committed by its own employees. This translates into about $600 billion in 2002—more than four times the tangible losses from street crime shown in Table 3.3 (even adjusting for inflation, the $105 billion in tangible losses in 1993 shown in Table 3.3 translates into about $130 billion in 2002). Over half of the frauds reported caused losses of at least $100,000, with nearly one in six causing losses of $1 million or more. Small businesses are apparently very vulnerable to occupational fraud—presumably owing to lack of internal controls.

*Table 3.6* Rate of victimization (per 1,000 population) per year by crime by household income

| Household income | All serious violent crime | Rape and sexual assault | Robbery | Aggravated assault |
|---|---|---|---|---|
| Combined | 30.6 | 1.1 | 2.2 | 4.3 |
| Less than $7,500 | 45.5 | 2.5 | 6.3 | 11.2 |
| $7,500–14,999 | 31.2 | 3.2 | 4.1 | 5.8 |
| $15,000–24,999 | 30.1 | 2.1 | 2.9 | 6.1 |
| $25,000–34,999 | 27.0 | 1.2 | 2.9 | 4.1 |
| $35,000–49,999 | 25.6 | 0.9 | 2.2 | 5.2 |
| $50,000–74,999 | 18.7 | 0.3 | 2.1 | 2.5 |
| $75,000 + | 19.0 | 0.2 | 1.0 | 2.8 |

Source: Figures based on average victimization rates in 2002 taken from BJS (2004b: Table 14, "Victimization rates for persons age 12 and over, and by type of crime and annual family income of victims").

The average occupational fraud reported against a small business caused $127,500 in losses compared to $97,000 in average losses for larger companies. It is important to note, however, that the ACFE study is not a nationally representative random sample of companies. It is also based on what the author terms "subjective" assessment of the fraud problem as reported by certified auditors.

Table 3.8 lists various estimates of the cost of white-collar or economic crimes. For example, Titus, Heinzelmann, and Boyle (1995) conducted a national survey of the U.S. population to identify victims of personal fraud. They estimated the annual tangible costs to be $45 billion. However, some of the fraud definitions include incidents that may not be considered criminal. This highlights an important definitional issue when it comes to economic and regulatory crimes. Unlike street crime, oftentimes fraud and regulatory violations can be classified as civil, regulatory, or criminal—and the decision about how to label the incident is largely up to the prosecutor. Large corporate scandals are often settled by the government in the civil arena even though they might have been prosecuted criminally. Whether or not adequate evidence of criminal intent or culpability could be established is not the only criterion by which a prosecutor might determine whether to charge with a criminal violation. Other factors that might come into play include the burden or cost of proving criminal intent and the willingness of corporate officials to "settle" the case if criminal charges are not pursued. In addition, the standards of corporate criminal liability in the U.S. are such that "intent" does not necessarily have to be shown as it does in most criminal charges filed against an individual. Thus there is likely to be considerably more discretion in whether or not to prosecute a corporation as opposed to

*Table 3.7* Rate of violent victimization (per 1,000 population) per year by race, gender, and age

| Race and age of victim | Male | | | | Female | | | |
|---|---|---|---|---|---|---|---|---|
| | Violent offenses | Rob-bery | Aggrav. assault | Simple assault | Violent offenses | Rob-bery | Aggrav. assault | Simple assault |
| **White** | | | | | | | | |
| Combined | 25.4 | 2.5 | 5.2 | 17.5 | 20.3 | 1.4 | 3.1 | 6.0 |
| 12–15 | 49.2 | 3.8 | 5.7 | 39.6 | 45.8 | 1.2 | 4.9 | 35.6 |
| 16–19 | 61.9 | 4.9 | 15.8 | 40.2 | 51.0 | 3.5 | 5.8 | 35.9 |
| 20–24 | 56.4 | 7.2 | 14.0 | 34.7 | 42.9 | 2.2 | 8.4 | 26.5 |
| 25–34 | 30.5 | 3.2 | 6.0 | 21.1 | 22.3 | 1.8 | 3.6 | 15.7 |
| 35–49 | 18.9 | 1.9 | 3.3 | 13.5 | 17.8 | 0.9 | 3.3 | 13.1 |
| 50–64 | 10.8 | 1.0 | 1.9 | 7.8 | 9.9 | 1.3 | 1.3 | 7.2 |
| 65 + | 3.1 | 0.2 | 1.4 | 1.5 | 2.6 | 0.8 | 0.0 | 1.6 |
| **Black** | | | | | | | | |
| Combined | 29.0 | 5.7 | 7.4 | 15.1 | 27.0 | 2.7 | 6.0 | 14.3 |
| 12–15 | 40.2 | 8.5 | 5.3 | 26.3 | 38.8 | 0.0 | 3.9 | 28.5 |
| 16–19 | 50.6 | 6.2 | 24.7 | 19.7 | 96.1 | 2.5 | 17.8 | 40.5 |
| 20–24 | 50.7 | 6.5 | 13.3 | 30.9 | 22.4 | 0.0 | 2.5 | 17.3 |
| 25–34 | 31.7 | 5.1 | 12.3 | 14.4 | 32.0 | 6.1 | 6.7 | 17.9 |
| 35–49 | 19.8 | 3.7 | 2.8 | 11.8 | 19.4 | 0.8 | 8.6 | 9.4 |
| 50–64 | 19.1 | 6.4 | 3.0 | 7.6 | 10.7 | 4.1 | 0.7 | 5.9 |
| 65 + | 12.1 | 7.7 | 0.0 | 4.4 | 7.3 | 4.7 | 2.6 | 0.0 |

Source: Figures based on average victimization rates in 2002 taken from BJS (2004b: Table 10, "Violent crimes, 2002: Number of victimizations and victimization rates for persons age 12 and over, by race, gender, and age of victims and type of crime").

an individual. It is therefore not always clear how recent corporate scandals such as the $1.4 billion settlement in the mutual fund industry or the $400 million settlement by Worldcom should be classified. Are these scandals—handled in the civil arena—any different from the criminal conspiracy charges in a Medicaid overbilling scheme settled for $437 million by Abbott Laboratories' TAP Pharmaceutical Products Inc.? In fact, there are numerous similar government overcharge cases that are settled without criminal charges. One simple way is to include only offenses where criminal sanctions are imposed. But that would result in an underestimate of the true cost of corporate and white-collar crime. While I am unaware of any attempt to aggregate the total cost of corporate fraud, several websites now attempt to list all known instances of monetary fines and penalties for "corporate crime"—broadly construed to include civil penalties and settlements (see, for example, http://www.endgame.org/corpfines.html).

Noticeably missing from Table 3.8 are many regulatory offenses such as anti-trust, environmental, and food and drug. Few government agencies attempt to estimate the social or external costs—and even when they do,

*Table 3.8* The cost of criminal fraud

| Industry | Fraud type | Cost ($ billions) | Year | Source |
|---|---|---|---|---|
| All firms | Employee theft and fraud | 600 | 2002 | (1) |
| Telecommunications | Theft of services | 3.7–5.0 | 1995 | (2) |
| Health care | Overcharge, services not rendered, kickbacks, etc. | 70 | 1992 | (3) |
| Insurance | False claims | 120 | 1995 | (4) |
| Entertainment | Bootlegging | 2.3 | 1995 | (5) |
| Telemarketing | Con artists, sweepstakes, phone scams | up to 40 | 1995 | (6) |
| All consumers | Fraud in general | 45 | 1991 | (7) |

Sources:

1   Association of Certified Fraud Examiners (2002).
2   Communications Fraud Association. Private communication.
3   U.S. General Accounting Office (1992).
4   Insurance Information Institute (1996).
5   Recording Industry Association of America as cited in Reuter (1996).
6   Federal Trade Commission (1998).
7   Titus, Heinzelmann, and Boyle (1995).

they are less than comprehensive. Based on the relatively large fines, cleanup costs, etc. that can accrue in these cases, these regulatory crimes have the potential for enormous costs. For example, following their conviction on criminal charges in the *Exxon Valdez* oil spill off the coast of Alaska, the company reportedly paid over $8 billion in cleanup costs, fines, and other monetary penalties (Jones, Jones, and Phillips-Patrick, 1994)—not to mention billions more in potential punitive damages (which have little to do with the harm caused). On the other hand, some regulatory crimes are primarily reporting requirements that involve little harm (Cohen, 1989).

More recent forms of crime involve computer-related incidents such as theft of proprietary information, sabotage of data networks, insider abuse of networks, denial of service, viruses, and laptop theft. While many of these crimes would be covered by the categories above, some—such as viruses and sabotage—might not. A recent survey by the Computer Security Institute (Richardson, 2003) of 530 computer security practitioners in U.S. corporations, government agencies, and non-profit institutions found total estimated losses of $200 million in 2003. This figure has not been extrapolated to the entire population of U.S. firms.

One conceptual difficulty in estimating the cost of crime against business is how to value the items taken. If money is taken, the value is straightforward—the face value of the bills. However, if the loss is merchandise, whether the loss should be valued at retail or wholesale depends on the opportunity cost to the victim. If the victim can easily replenish the product as needed and does not lose retail sales, the loss is the cost to the owner—

not the price at which it would sell. However, if the item is scarce and cannot be readily replaced, the loss is now the full value the owner could have expected to receive. Some white-collar crimes involve theft of services that involve essentially zero marginal costs to the victim and might not have been purchased at all in the absence of the theft. For example, the telecommunications industry estimates it is defrauded out of $3.7 to $5 billion per year in schemes that allow users to obtain free services. This is only a loss to the phone company, however, if the user would have actually purchased the service in the absence of the theft. If these services would not have been purchased, it is hard to label this a "cost." This is particularly true with "bootlegged" music and counterfeit luxury goods. Of course, in all cases, there may be other more subtle costs associated with the loss, such as diminishing the value of the legitimate product to all law-abiding purchasers.

There have also been numerous estimates of the cost of fraud outside the U.S. However, different definitions and methodologies make any comparison across countries difficult if not impossible. Brand and Price (2001) estimate that the total cost of public-sector fraud (e.g. tax fraud or fraudulent claims for social welfare benefits) plus commercial fraud (e.g. credit card fraud) was £10.3 billion. This compares to about £25 billion that was estimated to be the cost to victims of street crime. Thus while commercial crime alone in the U.S. is estimated to be more than four times the tangible costs of street crime, the estimate in the U.K. is that it is less than a quarter of the tangible cost of street crime. I would view these vast differences as being illustrative of the fact that the commercial fraud estimates are not comparable—not necessarily that fraud in the U.S. is far worse a problem than in the U.K.

To date I am unaware of any study that attempts to quantify the intangible costs of fraud. In addition, the studies to date have assumed that the tangible losses are limited to the dollar value of the fraud. Nevertheless, there is anecdotal evidence that losses can be significantly greater in certain cases. For example, some frauds prey on the elderly and uneducated poor. To the extent that these victims lose their homes, are unable to afford health care, etc., the costs may far exceed the dollar value of the fraud. Whether or not these losses are common or significant in the aggregate is unknown.

Some crimes with very large intangible costs, like treason or crimes that betray the public trust, may never be monetized. Nevertheless, we can conceptualize the "social cost" of these crimes. For example, the social cost of treason might be thought of as the risk of harm to our national security. However, quantifying that risk and the possible harm is another matter. Cohen (1989) examines the social costs associated with numerous types of corporate crime, including fraud, environmental, food and drug, safety, and export violations and other regulatory offenses. Although it is difficult to estimate social costs for some of these crimes, the vast majority of corporate crimes are frauds that can be easily measured, and techniques exist for estimating the harm in many other instances.

## Drug crimes

Estimating the cost of drug crimes is particularly difficult. To some economists, drug abuse is nothing more than a "victimless" crime, which is not by itself an external cost if the user voluntarily purchases drugs and reaps the full benefits and costs associated with use. Nevertheless, drug abuse imposes many external costs: drug users might be less productive in the workforce and might commit crimes to support their drug habits; dealers might forgo socially productive work activities; society might be burdened with additional medical costs in treating drug addicts.[10] Some of these costs (such as crime committed to support a drug habit and medical costs associated with drug overdoses) are clearly external and/or social costs irrespective of whether or not drug use is illegal. However, some costs are only social costs because society has deemed drug use to be illegal. For example, economists generally consider the forgone legitimate earnings of a person in the illegal drug trade to be a social cost owing to the socially valuable resources that are wasted. However, since illegal drug sales are voluntary transactions between two parties, these resources would not be considered social costs if drugs were made legal.

A series of reports have been commissioned by U.S. government agencies to determine the economic costs of drug abuse in the U.S. The most recent study, Office of National Drug Control Policy (ONDCP, 2001) estimates the total cost of drug abuse to be $143.4 billion in 1998. The bulk of these costs ($98.5 billion) are productivity losses to drug abusers, including premature death, reduced productivity while at work, career criminals not entering the legitimate labor market, and crime-related costs such as victim losses and time spent by offenders who are incarcerated. About $12.9 billion is estimated to be spent on drug-abuse services and health care for drug-related illnesses. The remaining $32.1 billion is estimated to be the cost of crime committed by drug abusers. ONDCP (2001) only includes tangible costs and ignores intangible costs to victims, families of drug abusers, etc. Since a significant portion of these costs are associated with victims of crime, there is some overlap between these estimates and those reported in Miller, Cohen, and Wiersema (1996).

The ONDCP (2001) report illustrates the difficulty of preparing credible estimates of the cost of drug abuse. First, the empirical evidence on the causal connection between drug abuse and crime is limited and largely unresolved (Miczek *et al.*, 1994). Thus the authors necessarily rely on assumptions that are based on a few limited studies. In addition, they assume average productivity losses for incarcerated drug offenders are the same as average productivity for workers in the population (see Cohen, 1999). Yet we know that the typical incarcerated offender is not as productive as the average person in the population (Cohen, Miller, and Rossman, 1993), and those engaged in street-level drug dealing have been found to have relatively low legitimate wage-earning potential (Reuter, MacCoun, and Murphy, 1990).

The actual cost of purchasing illegal drugs is not included in the ONDCP (2001) study. According to a study by Abt Associates (1995), about $53 billion was spent on illegal drugs in 1992.[11] Heavy cocaine users are estimated to spend about $9,000 to $10,000 per year on cocaine and heroin addicts spend about $17,000 per year (ONDCP, 1991). However, adding these costs would largely result in double counting. Drug users buying drugs transfer wealth from themselves to the seller which is a voluntary transaction not resulting in direct external costs. However, significant external and social costs do result from the activities surrounding the purchase and consumption of drugs (i.e. theft to support a drug habit, medical costs associated with drug-induced illness, etc.). Cohen (1998: 19) argues that one could use the cost of drugs as a proxy for the opportunity cost of resources devoted to drug distribution. However, there is a significant risk premium associated with selling drugs, which presumably is reflected in the price of drugs. Noting that the Reuter, MacCoun, and Murphy (1990) study of street-level drug dealers finds legitimate hourly earnings to be about 25 percent of hourly earnings from drug sales, in Cohen (1998) I assumed as a first approximation that only 25 percent of the price of drugs represents a social cost—the lost productivity owing to a drug dealer not working in legitimate activities. The remainder represents a risk premium paid to dealers who must face a higher risk of being killed on the job.

The British Home Office recently commissioned a study that estimated the cost of drug abuse in England and Wales (Godfrey *et al.* 2002). That study put the annual social cost of drug abuse caused by heavy drug users at between £10–35 billion. This figure included health costs, lost productivity, and the cost of the criminal justice system. The latter only included the cost of processing and incarcerating drug dealers and drug abusers—it does not include street crimes that presumably were caused by a need to support a drug habit. Given differing methodologies and assumptions, it would once again be difficult if not impossible to compare these estimates to the estimates prepared in the U.S.

Finally, the United Nations has an ongoing project to estimate the worldwide flow of illegal drug money. They estimate the total consumer sales of illicit drugs to be about $400 billion in 1995 (United Nations, 1998)—a figure that is about eight times the Abt Associates (1995) estimate of sales in the U.S. Thus U.S. illicit drug sales would represent about 12 percent of worldwide consumption. The U.N. report notes that $400 billion is about 8 percent of total international trade, and is approximately the same size as world tourism, and six times the amount spent on official development assistance worldwide.

# 4 Third-party and society costs

While crime has its most dramatic impact on victims, others suffer as well. Family members of crime victims may have to take time off work to accompany a victim to the doctor or otherwise care for the victim. They may grieve over the loss of a loved one and may themselves require psychological counseling to deal with such a loss or simply to deal with the trauma of having a family member victimized. Children of domestic violence victims may suffer long-lasting psychological effects that can only be overcome with costly treatment and long-term care. Others may also suffer, such as the employer who needs to hire a replacement worker or pay workers overtime while an injured victim is off the job. Society as a whole, either as insurance purchasers or as taxpayers, may bear some of these costs through higher insurance premiums or higher taxes. Some of these costs (e.g. administrative costs of insurance) are in addition to victim costs. Others (e.g. higher insurance premiums to cover additional crime-related losses) are simply a shifting of the cost burden from the victim to a larger group of people. Taxpayers pay for crime prevention and criminal justice programs. Potential victims—including virtually every member of society—pay through increased security or changing their behavior in ways that represent increased time or a decrease in pleasurable activities such as walking in a park.

Third-party costs are perhaps the least studied component of the cost of crime. In this chapter we explore some of these third-party costs in detail. Third-party and society costs generally fall into the same categories identified in Table 1.1: (a) costs directly attributable to individual crimes, (b) costs of society's response to crime, and (c) offender costs. Each is dealt with in turn. In addition, however, there is growing awareness that trying to piece together all of these individual costs is a difficult task that will likely underestimate the true impact of crime. At the end of this chapter, we will explore a relatively new approach to estimating costs that attempts to assess the aggregate burden of crime by developing an understanding of society's willingness to pay to reduce crime.

## Costs directly attributable to individual crimes

In this section we consider third-party costs that are directly attributable to individual criminal episodes. Thus, we examine the effect of victimization on family members of victims, on those who might witness a crime, on insurance companies (and ultimately all insurance purchasers) who pay many of the expenses associated with victimization, and on taxpayers who might also share many of these burdens.

### Family members and other non-victims directly affected by victimization

Family members can be affected by victim injuries in several different ways. First, they may be inconvenienced through increased household chores and attending to the needs of the victim while the victim is recovering. Second, there may be a psychic cost or "loss of companionship." Finally, family members who witness the victimization may suffer actual psychological trauma. In some cases, victimization might have a psychological impact on other third parties outside the immediate family of the victim.

### Lost productivity to family members

I am unaware of any data on the amount of time spent by family members attending to the needs of crime victims. While the NCVS asks victims how much time they spent dealing with the criminal justice system or losing time at work, no questions of that nature are asked of family members. Presumably, for most criminal victimizations, this amount is likely to be less than the amount that victims themselves suffer. Thus one could approximate these losses by assuming that they are no greater than lost productivity suffered by crime victims. Of course, one would want to value the lost hours by the care-giver's wage rate, not the wage rate of the victim. If the care-giver is a parent who works and the victim is a child in school, the third-party losses might be considerably higher than the direct victim losses. On the other hand, some crimes will not involve any care-giver, or will involve one whose marginal value of time is less than the victim's time. Thus without further study this is largely a hidden cost of crime.

### Loss of services to family members

Loss of companionship is probably more relevant in death cases than in injury cases. However, this problem may also occur in injury cases— especially those with severe injury, sexual assault, and rape. Although I am unaware of any studies that attempt to quantify or assess the magnitude of these losses to family members of crime victims, there is ample evidence that

*Table 4.1* Jury awards for loss of services to family members of injury or death victims ($)

| Injury | Injury to wife | Injury to husband | Injury to parent of minor child |
|---|---|---|---|
| Soft tissue injury | 5,000 | 10,000 | 3,500 |
| Strains, sprains | 4,900 | 5,000 | 2,950 |
| Concussions, dental injuries | 5,500 | 5,500 | 3,500 |
| Fracture or organ damage with no permanent injury | 10,000 | 25,000 | 23,675 |
| Fracture or organ damage with permanent impairment | 15,000 | 25,000 | 40,000 |
| Mild brain injuries or single limb amputations | 55,000 | 100,000 | 25,000 |
| Severe brain damage, multiple limb amputations or paralysis | 550,000 | 287,931 | 650,000 |
| Sexual assault, molestation, child abuse | 100,000 | – | 150,000 |
| Emotional distress or PTSD | 25,000 | 26,250 | 125,000 |
| Death | 150–400,000 | 118–350,000 | 650,000 |

Source: LRP Publications (2001). All figures are medians.

these losses can be real. For example, in many states, spouses, or children of accident or death victims, may sue a negligent party for loss of services.

A recent nationwide study of jury awards examined awards for loss of services, which were defined to include "the loss of society, affection, help, comfort, guidance, and/or conjugal relations that the injured or deceased person was not able to provide" (LRP Publications, 2001: 4.50.2). As shown in Table 4.1, these losses are relatively small for minor injuries such as soft tissue injuries, strains, sprains, or concussions—generally about $5,000 or less. However, reported median awards to spouses or children whose parents suffer severe brain injury or paralysis can be substantial— from $287,900 for injury to a husband, $550,000 for injury to a wife, and $650,000 for injury to a parent. Awards to spouses of a family member who was killed range from $150,000 to $400,000, while loss to a minor child for a parent who dies averages $650,000. Note that these losses are based on all types of victimization—whether they are caused by an accident or by crime.

However, one category of the LRP Publications (2001) study specifically related to certain types of criminal victimization—sexual assault, molestation, and child abuse. The median award to a husband whose wife is sexually assaulted is $100,000, while the loss to a parent of a child who is assaulted is $150,000. Note that these losses are only valid to the extent that the injury was severe enough—and the loss to the surviving family members devastating enough—to warrant filing and winning compensation in a lawsuit. Thus it would not be appropriate to assume these losses for all criminal victimizations where there is a surviving spouse or child.

Although the awards to family members in the case of catastrophic injury (including death) are extremely large, it would not necessarily be reasonable to add these to the cost-of-crime estimates shown in Chapter 3—especially in the case of murder. As discussed in Chapter 3, the estimated cost of a murder is based on willingness to pay to avoid the risk of death. This value is based primarily on wage-rate differentials for risky jobs. Since the entire family shares a wage earner's salary, the willingness-to-pay amount is likely to represent the loss to a family unit. Thus to count these losses to family members might be double counting.

### Psychological impacts on family members and other non-victims

Apart from any loss of services, there might be psychological injury to a family member who witnesses victimization. Pynoos and Eth (1985: 22) report that children directly view a mother being raped in about 10 percent of all rapes reported to the police in Los Angeles County. Nationally, they report that about 40 percent of all rapes occur at home, and that 40 percent of all rape victims are of child-bearing age. In addition, they report that a child witnessed or knew about marital rape in 11 percent of these incidents.

Pynoos and Eth (1985: 20) report "nearly 80 percent of the over 100 uninjured child witnesses (to the murder of a parent, rape of a mother, or suicidal act of a parent) we studied also exhibited a characteristic pattern of PTSD." Although this is not a random sample and we do not know the selection method for inclusion in their study, it would not be surprising to find such high rates of psychological injury in these cases.

Pynoos and Eth (1985: 21) also report that "the Sheriff's Homicide Division of Los Angeles County estimates that dependent children witness between 10 to 20 percent of the approximately 2,000 annual homicides in their jurisdiction." They go on to claim that virtually all of the 50 child homicide witnesses they interviewed experienced PTSD (p. 29).

Although few studies have tried to assess the long-term mental health consequences to the family of a victim of crime, a good deal of literature describes the mental health effects on spouses and parents of victims of other causes of sudden death. The recovery process is apparently much slower when the victim suffered an unexpected death as opposed to being forewarned (such as in chronic illness).

Lehman, Wortman, and Williams (1987) compared a sample of 80 individuals who had lost a spouse or child in a motor vehicle crash from 4 to 7 years earlier, to a matched control group of 80 similar individuals who had not experienced this type of loss, as well as to national norms and a group of female psychiatric outpatients. Based on a series of questions designed to assess psychological well-being, they found that the bereaved group reported rates of depression that were 20–30 percent higher than the control group.

Another survey of 214 family members of homicide victims and 105 non-victim controls (drawn from a random sample of 12,500 U.S. adults) found that 23.4 percent of family members of homicide victims developed homicide-related PTSD at some time following the death (Amick-McMullan, Kilpatrick, and Veronen, 1989 and Kilpatrick, Resnick, and Amick, 1989). However, "in terms of general psychological distress, survivors were no more symptomatic than non-victim controls." Although not stated by the authors, this finding suggests that most family members who did develop PTSD substantially recovered prior to the interview.

According to a study by Kilpatrick and Saunders (1997), 43 percent of male adolescents and 35 percent of female adolescents had witnessed some form of violence firsthand. Fifteen percent of those who had witnessed violence developed PTSD, compared to 3 percent of surveyed youths who had not witnessed violence.

Cohen and Miller (1998) conducted a survey of mental health care providers to determine the extent to which they treat crime victims. This survey was discussed in Chapter 3, and some of the empirical findings were reported in Table 3.4. One of the categories of crime was "witnessing a murder or losing a loved one to murder." Surprisingly, this category turned out to involve the highest incidence of mental health care per victim. Cohen and Miller estimated that, on average, a murder results in between 1.5 and 2.0 family members or others seeking mental health care treatment primarily as a result of the victimization, with the average cost per person treated being $2,330 in 1991 dollars. Of course, these costs are only the cost of mental health care treatment itself, and exclude the value of any lost productivity to the patient and the value of any pain, suffering, and lost quality of life they suffer.

In addition to family members, other witnesses of violent behavior might suffer from psychological trauma—especially in cases of severe injury or death. According to data compiled from the NCVS, 69 percent of all violent crimes were witnessed by more than one person—either additional victims, family members or bystanders (BJS, 1989: 4). Unfortunately, we do not know the percentage in each witness category. One measure of the cost of an individual incidence of witnessing a violent crime is the compensatory damage award in lawsuits brought on behalf of such witnesses. According to LRP Publications (2001: 5.80.2), the median jury award to a plaintiff who witnesses a physical assault and suffers psychological trauma as a result is $10,000. This figure is higher for witnessing a death—although it is not clear what the exact figure is. The median award for witnessing all injuries and deaths—not only resulting from criminal victimization but also from accidents—is $33,250.

### Insurance payments

Many of the direct costs of crime have already been identified and estimated in Chapter 3—even for those that are borne by third parties. Medical costs are often paid for by insurance companies or government programs, or hospitals themselves when a victim is indigent. Thus, even though those costs might be included in Chapter 3, many of them are really borne by third parties who are not direct victims.

In the case of losses that are covered by medical or homeowners' insurance, total costs exceed direct victim losses because there are additional overhead costs associated with these programs. If an injured party submits a medical claim with her insurance company, the company incurs a cost of processing that claim. Miller, Cohen, and Wiersema (1996) report that overhead costs average 16 percent for property insurance, 7.5 percent for medical insurance, and 13 percent for workers' compensation that covers lost wages. They include these overhead costs in their cost per victimization, and hence they are included in Chapter 3 as well. Many—but not all—victim losses are likely to be covered by insurance. For example, about 70 percent of homeowners have property insurance and over 80 percent have medical insurance. However, to the extent that victimization occurs more frequently among lower income populations, insurance coverage might be less comprehensive.

Miller, Cohen, and Wiersema (1996) estimate that in 1993, $45 billion in out-of-pocket expenses were paid for by insurance companies. As shown in Table 4.2, more than half of this amount ($25.1 billion) went to compensate victims of drunk-driving accidents—including both automobile damage and medical costs to victims. Table 4.2 reports on the amount of insurance payments estimated to be paid out to victims of crime. This is compared both to the tangible victim costs of crime (e.g. medical care, lost wages, property

*Table 4.2* Percentage of crime victim costs reimbursed by insurance

| Type of crime | Amount reimbursed by insurance (£) | Tangible costs (£) | Total costs (£) | % of tangible costs reimbursed | % of total costs reimbursed |
|---|---|---|---|---|---|
| Murder | 1.2 | 33.4 | 93.0 | 3.6 | 1.3 |
| Child sex abuse | 0.6 | 2.3 | 23.0 | 26.1 | 2.6 |
| Other child abuse | 0.8 | 5.1 | 33.0 | 15.7 | 2.4 |
| Rape (excl. child sex abuse) | 1.7 | 7.5 | 127.0 | 22.7 | 1.3 |
| Other assault | 3.3 | 15.0 | 93.0 | 22.0 | 3.5 |
| Robbery | 0.5 | 3.1 | 11.0 | 16.1 | 4.5 |
| Drunk-driving | 25.1 | 13.4 | 41.0 | 187.3 | 61.2 |
| Arson | 2.4 | 2.7 | 5.0 | 88.9 | 48.0 |
| Larceny | 2.1 | 9.1 | 9.0 | 23.1 | 23.3 |
| Burglary | 3.5 | 7.0 | 9.0 | 50.0 | 38.9 |
| Motor vehicle theft | 3.6 | 6.3 | 7.0 | 57.1 | 51.4 |
| Total | 45.0 | 105.0 | 450.0 | 42.7 | 10.0 |

Source: Miller, Cohen, and Wiersema (1996: Tables 5 and 8). Based on 1993 data.

Note: Figures may not add owing to rounding.

losses) and to the total victim costs (including pain, suffering, and lost quality of life). For example, reimbursement to families of murder victims totaled about $1.2 billion, compared to tangible costs of $33.4 billion and total costs of $93.0 billion. Thus insurance reimbursement amounted to only about 3.6 percent of tangible costs and 1.3 percent of total costs. For many crimes, however, the insurance payout is considerably higher. For example, approximately 50 percent of the tangible losses from burglary are covered by insurance. Insurance covers an even higher portion of tangible losses for motor vehicle theft (57.1 percent), and arson (88.9 percent). Drunk-driving is an unusual situation, with total insurance payments far exceeding tangible costs (187.3 percent of tangible costs) and amounting to 61.2 percent of total costs. The reason this figure is so high is that most drunk-driving offenders have insurance (or are covered by uninsured motor vehicle insurance) and thus most victims can recover costs. Moreover, in no-fault states, even offenders can be reimbursed for their losses.

Table 4.3 reports on the percentage of total insurance payouts in the U.S. that are estimated to be the direct result of criminal victimization. In the case of health insurance, life insurance, and workers' compensation, crime victim losses represent only a very small part of insurance company payouts— about 2 percent. However, they represent a very significant portion of both auto insurance payouts (28.9 percent) as a result of both motor vehicle theft and drunk-driving accidents, and homeowners' insurance (37.9 percent) as a result of burglary and arson. These costs are borne by all policyholders—not just victims. Thus significant reductions in drunk-driving accidents, motor vehicle theft, burglary, and arson will have a financial impact on all drivers and homeowners who buy insurance. However, the impact of these crimes is not necessarily uniform across all policyholders. Homeowners who live in relatively high-crime areas may be charged higher insurance premiums. Automobile owners who own models that are frequently stolen or who live in cities with high motor vehicle theft rates will also be charged higher auto insurance premiums. Thus the effect of crime on insurance costs is likely to be spread somewhat disproportionately on policyholders based on their risk.

*Table 4.3* Percentage of insurance payments for crime-related losses

| Type of insurance | Payments ($ billion) | % of annual payments |
| --- | --- | --- |
| Health | 11.0 | 1.8 |
| Life | 1.5 | 2.2 |
| Workers' compensation | 1.0 | 2.2 |
| Auto | 23.5 | 28.9 |
| Homeowners' fire and theft | 7.9 | 37.9 |

Source: Miller, Cohen, and Wiersema (1996: Table 8). Based on 1993 data.

## Productivity losses to employers of victims

Although wage losses to victims were included in Chapter 3, those losses do not necessarily capture the full cost to society of lost productivity owing to crime. If victims are replaced with temporary help or overtime assistance from other workers, it might cost the employer more than the wages that would have otherwise gone to the victim. In some cases, an employer might pay both the victim (who is on sick leave, for example) and temporary or overtime help. Alternatively, the employer might simply forgo the productivity of the victim who is temporarily out of work. If the victim's productivity exceeds her wage rate, then this again would represent a loss to the employer that is beyond the wage rate itself. If the victim leaves employment altogether (e.g. is murdered or permanently disabled), the cost of hiring and training a replacement might be an additional loss to the employer. To date, I am unaware of any studies that have attempted to estimate these additional monetary costs of crime.

## Society's response to victimization

In Chapter 1, I enumerated a laundry list of the cost of society's response to victimization. These costs fall into three broad categories: crime prevention and avoidance, criminal justice programs, and incarcerated offender costs. A few additional costs fall outside these broad categories such as victim services (which were included in our discussion in Chapter 3) and the costs of justice and overdeterrence. Each of these categories will be dealt with below.

### Crime prevention and avoidance behavior

According to a recent Gallup poll, 32 percent of the American population reported in 2002 that they live within a mile of an area where they are "afraid to walk alone at night" (BJS, 2003a: Table 2.36). This figure is the lowest in many years, with a high of 47 percent being recorded in 1982. Not surprising, given their different risks of victimization and ability to defend themselves from attackers, fear of walking alone at night varies by age, sex, and race. For example, only 17 percent of males reported they were afraid to walk alone at night near their home, compared to 55 percent of females. Whites were also less afraid (36 percent) than blacks (50 percent). People who fear being crime victims are likely to change their behavior. They might take fewer walks at night, or buy more expensive locks and security systems etc. These are preventive measures designed to reduce the likelihood of victimization by reducing exposure to risky situations.

A survey of households in Washington, D.C. in 1971 (Clotfelter, 1977: 502), found the following reported rates of self-protective behavior:

| | |
|---|---|
| Usually lock house when at home | 84.9 percent |
| Usually leave lights on when away | 65.8 percent |
| Ever stay at home at night because of crime | 43.8 percent |
| Installed additional locks | 42.7 percent |
| Ever take taxis because of crime | 28.6 percent |
| Carry something for protection | 15.0 percent |
| Obtained watchdog | 12.4 percent |
| Put bars on windows | 5.9 percent |
| Installed burglar alarm | 2.7 percent |

As the Clotfelter study makes clear, some of our responses to crime involve actual dollar outlays—such as purchasing burglar alarms or guard dogs—while others involve "opportunity costs" such as locking doors or staying home at night because of fear of crime. Estimating the magnitude of these costs is difficult in both cases. In the case of direct outlays, it is often the case that expenditures are made for multiple purposes. Thus, for example, a guard dog might also provide companionship, and purchase of a firearm might be for purposes of both protection and sport. Sorting out the marginal cost owing to crime is thus difficult.

Quantifying opportunity costs involves additional complexity, since we do not actually pay money when we lock a door or walk a longer distance to avoid a high-crime area. Economists generally value time by assuming it is equal to the wage rate at which the individual could earn money if she was not spending time on that activity. Thus the opportunity cost of time spent in a crime prevention activity is estimated as forgone earnings for the same length of time. This is true even if an individual would not actually work in the absence of spending time on crime prevention. Even if that time were spent on leisure activities, economists would note that the leisure activity is thus valued at least as high as the forgone earnings.

One of the most comprehensive attempts to estimate third-party costs of crime was conducted by Anderson (1999). Anderson tallied up what he called "the costs of crime-induced production." This includes both what I have called the cost of "society's response to crime" and other direct victimization costs such as medical care for victims and other out-of-pocket losses. He also estimated "opportunity costs" of crime which include the value of time lost by both victims and potential victims. In this chapter we are only interested in the cost to potential victims as well as the cost to society in general—since we already estimated the cost to victims in Chapter 3. Thus Table 4.4 reproduces Anderson's estimates excluding the costs to victims. Excluding the costs to victims, the out-of-pocket costs in Anderson (1999) total $225.8 billion in 1999, while opportunity costs total $90.3 billion.

The bulk of out-of-pocket expenditures are paid for directly by taxpayers as part of the criminal justice system, representing about half the total amount shown in Table 4.4. We will discuss the criminal justice system in the following section. In contrast, other costs are much smaller even if they

*Table 4.4* The cost of society's response to crime

| Spending category | $ billions |
|---|---|
| Out-of-pocket costs | |
| Criminal justice system | |
|   Police | 57.7 |
|   Corrections | 43.5 |
|   Prenatal exposure to cocaine and heroin | 28.1 |
|   Anti-crime components of federal agency budgets | 23.4 |
|   Judicial and legal services, state, and local | 21.6 |
| *Subtotal: criminal justice system* | *174.3* |
| Private security costs | |
|   Guards | 17.9 |
|   Drug control | 10.9 |
|   Alarm systems | 6.5 |
|   Passes for business access | 4.7 |
|   Locks, safes, and vaults | 4.4 |
|   Firearms | 2.2 |
|   Surveillance cameras | 1.5 |
|   Safety lighting | 1.5 |
|   Protective fences and gates | 1.2 |
|   Airport security | 0.4 |
|   Non-lethal weapons | 0.3 |
|   Guard dogs | 0.01 |
| *Subtotal: private security* | *51.5* |
| *Sub-total: out-of-pocket (combined)* | *225.8* |
| Time spent securing assets | 89.6 |
| Time spent on neighborhood watch programs | 0.7 |
| *Subtotal: opportunity costs* | *90.3* |
| **Total** | **316.1** |

are significant, such as $4.4 billion spent on locks, safes, and vaults and
$1.5 billion spent on safety lighting.

Anderson (1999) includes a staggering $28.1 billion as the annual cost of
caring for prenatal exposure to cocaine and heroin. The source of this estimate is Hay (1991), who cites government estimates of 100,000 babies per
year who were born exposed to cocaine. At the time, experts estimated the
cost of caring for these babies and thought the neurological damage suffered
would be irreversible. More recently, researchers have learned that brain
damage is not permanent and the cost is not as high. Moreover, fewer babies
are exposed each year now than in 1990. According to the National Institute
of Drug Abuse (NIDA, 1992), an estimated $407 million is spent annually
on extra hospital costs to treat drug-exposed infants. Additionally, NIDA
(1999) estimates the annual cost of providing educational services to crack
babies to be about $350 million. Combined, these figures are less than
$1 billion per year.

Perhaps the most surprising cost shown in Table 4.4 is the enormous opportunity cost estimated to result from simply having to lock our homes, offices, cars, etc.—$89.6 billion. Anderson (1999) obtains this estimate through a survey of households in which he asked how many times people lock and unlock items in their daily lives. He then observed how long it takes to unlock and lock different items and estimated that the average person in the U.S. spends two minutes per day on such activities. Valued at average wage rates in the U.S., the $89.6 billion figure is simply an estimate of the value of that lost time.

Although one could identify types of crime that are more likely to be pre-vented by certain types of private protection expenditure or opportunity cost, it is impossible to apportion most of these costs to individual crimes. For example, even though a private home alarm or guard dog might be purchased to protect against burglary, they also protect a homeowner who happens to be home during a burglary from robbery, assault, rape, and murder. Thus some of the expenditures on burglar alarms or guard dogs might be more properly attributable to attempts to prevent rapes or assaults by intruders in one's home. However, if one takes the view that the cost of burglary includes the risk of being home and further victimized, then expen-ditures on home security are indeed attributable to burglary.

## Criminal justice programs

As discussed above, the bulk of out-of-pocket expenditures estimated to be part of society's response to crime is paid for directly by taxpayers as part of the criminal justice system, including police ($57.7 billion), correc-tions ($43.5 billion), anti-crime components of federal government agencies ($23.4 billion), and judicial and legal services at the state and local level ($21.6 billion). Combined, these four categories represent about half the total of $316.1 billion tallied up in Table 4.4.

Once again, although it is useful to know how much we are spending on police or courts, this information alone tells us little about the proper alloca-tion of tax dollars across these spending categories. What we would like to know is how much of the estimated $57.7 billion devoted to police is spent on armed robberies versus burglaries? What is the cost of police, courts, and corrections per armed robbery? Answers to these questions would help policymakers judge the effectiveness of current and proposed programs designed to reduce crime.

One approach to disentangling the cost of individual crimes is to take a "bottom-up" approach. For example, Cohen, Miller, and Rossman (1993: 126–34) attempted to piece together the cost of the criminal justice system on a "per crime" basis from a few studies done in single localities. They esti-mated the criminal justice processing cost "per offense" in 1987 dollars to be $5,925 for murder, $2,050 for rape, $1,125 for robbery, and $1,225 for aggravated assault. This includes the estimated cost of police investigations, and court-related costs such as pretrial booking and jail, hearings, and trials. I am unaware of any similar attempts to estimate per crime criminal justice costs for other crimes. Note that the appropriate "unit of analysis" is an issue that becomes important in such studies. Criminal investigation costs only occur for crimes reported to police. However, since not all crimes result in arrests or convictions, few other criminal justice costs occur unless an actual offender is apprehended. Thus, for example, although the estimated cost of processing an aggravated assault was estimated to be $1,225, the cost per victimization was only $580. However, since only 28.1 percent of aggravated assaults that were reported to police were cleared by arrest, the cost per arrested offender is considerably higher—about $4,400 in 1987 (Cohen, Miller, and Rossman, 1993: Tables 19–20).

Care must also be taken that one does not double-count the costs estimated in this chapter with victim costs estimated in Chapter 3. For example, both police and firefighters often provide emergency response to victimization. According to Miller, Cohen, and Wiersema (1996), dispatching emergency vehicles costs on average about $200 per incident for most crimes. The emergency responses to arson and murder are higher, about $1,000 to $2,000. These costs were included in Chapter 3 as being part of the "cost of victimization," since they are incurred primarily to assist victims—regardless of whether the incident was an accident or intentional victimization. In contrast, police investigation costs are more properly considered to be outside the cost of victimization itself and are instead part of "society's response to victimization."

## Offender costs

In addition to paying for the cost of incarceration, society loses the productive capacity of individuals who are incarcerated. These productivity losses are true social costs that should be taken into account when examining the costs and benefits of incarceration.

Only sparse data are available on the prior earnings history of incarcerated offenders. Sporadically, the Bureau of Justice Statistics conducts surveys of both local jails and state prisons. The last survey of jail inmates was conducted in late 1995 and early 1996, and included offenders who were sentenced to a term less than one year as well as those who were still awaiting trial, sentencing, or other legal dispositions. Thus some of these offenders might ultimately have been found to be innocent, while others might subsequently receive prison sentences longer than one year. According to the survey, 36 percent of all jail inmates were unemployed at the time of their incarceration (BJS, 1998). Of the 64 percent who were working, 49 percent had full-time jobs, while 15 percent had part-time or occasional jobs. This represents an employment rate that is below the average in the general population. For example, U.S. Department of Labor data for 1995 indicated that 74 percent of the U.S. population aged 18–64 were employed. The median income reported by jailed offenders was approximately $7,200 per year—which includes all legal and illegal sources of income and government assistance programs. Of course, this is self-report data and we do not know whether or not this amount is truly representative of income. Only 15 percent of jailed inmates admitted to having an illegal source of income.

The most recent survey of state prison inmates was conducted in 1991 (BJS, 1993). The findings are similar to that for jail inmates, with 67 percent working (55 percent full-time and 12 percent part-time). Median income was reportedly between $5,000 and $10,000 per year for all inmates who had been free for at least a year prior to their most recent incarceration. To combine the short-term jail inmates and the state prison inmates, I have updated them both to 2003 dollars and calculated the weighted average earnings reported by both jail and state inmates from these two surveys. This results in estimated average annual earnings of about $17,400 per offender. However, only a part of this income could be considered lost productivity owing to incarceration, because we do not know how much of this income was from productive labor versus other sources such as unemployment compensation, family members, social security disability, government welfare programs, or illegal sources. According to the jail inmate survey (BJS, 1998), only 74.7 percent of those who reported any income received wages. It was reported that 16.2 percent received money from family or friends, 15.2 percent from illegal sources, 13.8 percent from welfare, 6.6 percent from social security, and 8.6 percent from other sources including pensions, alimony, investment income, or unemployment compensation. These numbers add up to more than 100 percent because some offenders received income from multiple sources. In fact, by being incarcerated, some of these lost sources of income are actually social benefits—such as the reduction in illegal income and payments that do not have to be made from government welfare-type programs.

While some would also argue that the value of lost freedom to the offender should be considered (Becker, 1968: 179–80), others might question why we should care about the lost freedom to the offender when that is the purpose of incarceration. That is true if indeed one has decided upon incarceration as a sanction. However, if one is deciding whether to impose incarceration, it would be important to compare the cost of incarceration (which might include the lost productivity and the lost freedom to the offender) to the benefits of incarceration (which would include the value of incapacitating the offender and deterring others). Regardless of your feelings toward this approach, however, there are virtually no estimates of the value of lost freedom. In theory, one might be able to estimate the trade-off between fines and imprisonment by examining the rate of offenses in jurisdictions with different levels of fines and imprisonment (Posner, 1980: 413). However, I am unaware of any such studies. Moreover, it is not obvious that rich enough data exist to undertake such a study.

One possible measure of the value of lost freedom would be to examine jury awards for false imprisonment. Although false imprisonment data are not available, according to LRP Publications (2001), the mean award for false arrest by police is $85,000, with the median being $60,000.

In addition to the lost freedom from imprisonment, convicted felons are denied many civil rights such as voting, juror service, public employment, and firearm ownership (Burton, Cullen, and Travis, 1987). Once again, these might enter into part of the "benefits" side of the equation if they had either a deterrent or an incapacitative benefit.

One potential social cost of incarceration is the disruption of lives for the family of an offender. Incarceration no doubt places a financial and emotional burden on the remaining spouse and children. To some extent, these are "innocent victims" of the offense as well. Although few studies exist on the impact of incarceration on the family members of the offender, a significant percentage of incarcerated offenders have children. According to BJS (1993), there were 826,000 children in 1991 with one or more parent in a state prison; 67 percent of incarcerated women and 56 percent of men had at least one child. The vast majority of these children (94 percent) were being cared for by another parent or a grandparent.

It is also possible that sending offenders to jail will have the effect of "training" them to become more hardened criminals (Irwin and Austin, 1994: 17). To the extent that this is true, society incurs an additional cost associated with increased future criminal activity. This is a particularly difficult proposition to test empirically, as we do not generally permit randomized experiments in such criminal justice settings. One study of probation versus prison suggests prisoners have a slightly higher recidivism rate than similar probationers, but concludes, "the results presented here are only suggestive and should not be used to support specific policy recommendations" (Petersilia and Turner, 1986).

Finally, one potential cost associated with jailing offenders is the higher rate of injury and death while in prison. In 2000 the average prison population in state and federal facilities was approximately 1.2 million (BJS, 2003c). During the same year, the total number of suicides in these institutions was 198, a rate of 16.5 per 100,000 inmates. This compares to a nationwide suicide rate of about 10.4 per 100,000 residents. Another 56 inmate deaths were caused by other inmates, which represents a homicide rate of about 4.7 per 100,000 inmates. This compares to the nationwide homicide rate of 5.9 per 100,000. Thus, while it appears that inmate homicides are relatively rare, their suicide rate is more than 50 percent higher than the average population. However, it should be noted that both the suicide and homicide rates are significantly higher for males aged 18–44 (and particularly those between 25 and 34), which are also the groups with the highest criminal participation rates. Indeed, without a well-designed study, it is quite possible that prison—which often includes free mental health treatment—reduces the suicide rate among the affected population. Although I am unaware of studies directed specifically at these issues, Gaes (1985) reviews the existing literature on the effect of overcrowding on prison illness and violence. Without further study, we cannot conclude that jailed offenders have a higher rate of injury or death than their non-jailed cohorts.

## Willingness to pay to reduce crime

As discussed in Chapter 2, prior methodologies for estimating the costs of crime have largely relied upon estimating various components of crime costs and adding them together—such as victim medical costs, lost wages, police, and prison expenditures, and even intangible costs such as pain, suffering, and lost quality of life to victims. Presumably, society would be willing to pay at least this amount to avoid crime. However, we are also likely to pay more than this amount. Non-victims suffer from fear of crime and take costly actions to avoid being in a high-crime neighborhood or otherwise raise their risk of victimization. Neighborhood cohesiveness is reduced in a high-crime area as residents are afraid to go out at night. Society would benefit from crime reductions in many ways that go beyond the pure loss to victims. Thus, conceptually, when deciding whether or not to fund a program, we want to know how much the public expects to benefit—and hence how much they would be willing to pay for the program.

A few studies have begun to take this broader approach in valuing reductions in crime. As discussed in Chapter 2, one method of estimating the willingness to pay (WTP) for reduced crime is to use the "contingent valuation" (CV) methodology developed in the environmental economics literature to estimate WTP. The CV methodology has been used extensively to place dollar values on non-market goods such as improvements in air quality, saving endangered species, and reducing the risk of early death—social benefits that do not have direct market analogs. Although used in many different policy contexts, contingent valuation has not generally been employed in criminal justice research. Exceptions are Cook and Ludwig (2000) and Ludwig and Cook (2001), who use this method to estimate the amount that the average household would be willing to pay to reduce gun violence caused by criminals and juvenile delinquents. In these works it is estimated that the average household would be willing to pay about $200 per year to reduce gun violence caused by criminals and juvenile delinquents by 30 percent, which translates into about $1 million per injury. Similarly, Zarkin, Cates, and Bala (2000) report on a pilot study in which they use the CV method to value drug treatment programs.

More recently, Cohen *et al.* (2004) report on the results of a nationally representative survey of 1,300 U.S. adults, where information was solicited on their willingness to pay to reduce crime by 10 percent in their community. They found that the average household was willing to pay between $100 and $150 per year for crime prevention programs that reduced specific crimes by 10 percent in their communities. In the aggregate, these amounts imply a willingness to pay to prevent crime of about $25,000 per burglary,

*Table 4.5* Comparison of willingness to pay with previous estimates of crime costs

| Crime | *Prior estimates* | | | | |
| | *Victim costs($)* | *Criminal justice costs ($)* | *Total cost($)* | *WTP estimates ($)* | *Ratio WTP/ prior ($)* |
| --- | --- | --- | --- | --- | --- |
| Burglary | 1,780 | 2,580 | 4,360 | 25,000 | 5.7 |
| Armed robbery | 24,100 | 7,730 | 31,800 | 232,000 | 7.3 |
| Serious assaults | 30,480 | 5,150 | 35,600 | 70,000 | 2.0 |
| Rape and sexual assaults | 110,490 | 3,250 | 114,000 | 237,000 | 2.1 |
| Murder | 3,700,000 | 183,000 | 3,900,000 | 9,700,000 | 2.5 |

Source: Cohen, Rust, Steen, and Tidd (2004). All figures in 2000 dollars.

$70,000 per serious assault, $232,000 per armed robbery, $237,000 per rape and sexual assault, and $9.7 million per murder.

The more recent WTP estimates are more than twice the magnitude of earlier estimates that are based solely on the cost of crime to victims and criminal justice costs. As shown in Table 4.5, for example, the average victim cost of a burglary is estimated to be $1,780 in 2000 dollars (note that this is the same as the $1,400 figure in 1993 that is shown in Table 3.1). Criminal justice costs associated with the average burglary are estimated to be $2,580. This is based on the probability that a burglar will be caught, convicted, and sentenced, multiplied by the average cost of a burglary sentence. In other words, in response to the typical burglary, society on average spends $2,580 in criminal justice-related costs. Combined, the victim and criminal justice costs of an average burglary total $4,360. Yet society's willingness to pay appears to be much more—$25,000 per burglary. Presumably, this additional amount represents the increased sense of security, less need for burglar alarms, improvements in neighborhoods and economic development, and other benefits that accrue to non-victims of burglaries. Future studies that replicate and expand on the number of crimes would provide valuable insights into the true cost of crime to society.

# 5 Policy analysis and the costs of crime

As discussed briefly in Chapter 1, there are several reasons why criminal justice policymakers might be interested in quantifying the cost of crime. Thus policymakers might be interested in how crime compares to other social ills or whether the burden of crime on society is increasing or decreasing over time. One of the most important—and most controversial—purposes of placing dollar values on crime is to conduct a benefit–cost analysis.

Since the early 1980s, federal government regulatory agencies have been required to conduct benefit–cost analyses on major regulatory initiatives. These requirements have been adopted through Executive Order and implemented by the Office of Management and Budget.[1] Recent proposals in Congress would legislatively mandate similar requirements.[2] Thus benefit–cost analyses have become a routine tool in the development of environmental, health, and safety regulations.[3] Despite its widespread use elsewhere, benefit–cost analysis has not been a staple of the criminal justice policy analyst's toolkit. This is rapidly changing in response to both increasing public demand for accountability of government agencies and the availability of new data and techniques of analysis for identifying the costs and benefits of criminal justice policies. For example, the U.S. National Institute of Justice recently solicited research proposals in several priority topic areas. Among its priorities were "the studies that develop cost–benefit methods that can be applied to crime prevention or control programs or that assess the cost-effectiveness of specific crime prevention strategies, programs, and technologies" (NIJ, 2004). At the state level, legislatures in Washington, Oregon, Virginia, and others have begun to mandate studies of both "what programs work" and the cost-effectiveness (including weighing the costs and benefits) of criminal justice and crime prevention programs.[4] Ultimately, benefit–cost analyses might be required for newly proposed criminal justice policies.

The existing literature on benefits and costs of criminal justice policies generally takes either one of two forms: "cost-effectiveness" or "benefit–cost" studies. A cost-effectiveness study seeks to answer questions such as "what is the cost per crime averted?" or "what is the cost per successfully treated offender who does not recidivate?" These questions require a thorough understanding of costs and the probability of a successful outcome. They do not, however, require the analyst to monetize the successful outcome. To do so would be to conduct a "benefit–cost" analysis.

## Cost-effectiveness studies

To date, there have been few published studies of criminal justice or prevention programs that attempt to conduct either cost-effectiveness or benefit–cost analysis. Instead, researchers generally stop at the question of whether or not a certain punishment deters or whether a treatment program reduces recidivism at all. If so, the program "works." But at what cost? Are there alternative programs that would give us more "bang for our buck"?

A recent Congressionally mandated study focused on what empirical evidence exists that would shed light on which programs work and which do not (Sherman *et al.*, 1997). A team of researchers at the University of Maryland assessed hundreds of programs and program evaluations, including criminal justice, police, family-based programs such as early childhood interventions, and school prevention programs. This massive undertaking concluded that adequate data exist on some programs to determine whether or not they generally work. However, in many cases, there are not even adequate program evaluations to determine whether the program works. Interestingly, the study identified several programs that are continually funded despite growing evidence that they simply do not have any crime control benefits.

Assuming a program has been shown to reduce or prevent crime, some analysts go further and ask questions such as "what is the cost per treated offender?" Others go beyond this simple cost analysis and compare two or more programs using a "cost-effectiveness" approach. For example, a cost-effectiveness study might compare the cost per crime averted by a "three-strikes" policy that requires life in prison for a third-time felony offender versus that averted by a prevention program designed to reduce crime committed by at-risk youth. By finding the program that has the lowest cost per crime averted, one is able to find the most cost-effective program.

Greenwood *et al.* (1994) compare various incarceration alternatives considered during the "three-strikes" debate in California. In comparing five alternatives, the "cost per serious crime prevented" ranged from $11,800 (life in prison after the third violent offense) to $16,300 (life in prison after the third felony offense). Focusing only on violent offenders would thus appear to give us the most "bang for our buck," since we can achieve the same result for less money. However, incarcerating all third-time felons is likely to involve more offenders and hence reduce overall crime more than the alternative—even if the cost per crime averted is now higher. Since we do not know the value of the crimes averted, it is possible that the additional crime reduction from incarcerating all third-time felons is still worthwhile. That is, although we know that on a "per crime" basis, focusing on violent offenders is more cost-effective, this analysis cannot tell us which option is better.

Similarly, Greenwood *et al.* (1996) compared four child and youth intervention programs: home visits to new mothers and day care for their children, parent training, high school graduation incentives, and delinquent supervision. They found that per million dollars spent, graduation incentives prevented the largest number of serious crimes (258), followed by parent training (157), delinquent supervision (72), and home visit/day care (11). Thus, if we needed to choose between these programs to spend our next million dollars, it is clear that graduation incentives would provide the highest payoff. Although one might begin to prioritize spending on the basis of such a study, it does not tell us if *all* or only *some* of these programs should be adopted. For example, if the cost of 11 crimes exceeded $1 million, all of these options would be worth implementing. Similarly, if the cost of 258 serious crimes was less than $1 million, none of these options would be worth implementing from a benefit–cost perspective.

Thus, while the Greenwood *et al.* studies can help us determine which approach is most cost-effective, they are not equipped to determine whether any one approach is socially desirable. The policy analyst must make a subjective determination that the option being considered is worthwhile. That does not mean, however, that cost-effectiveness studies are without merit. As shown with the Greenwood *et al.* studies, cost-effectiveness may provide important information about the relative benefits of two or more programs being compared. As another example, Rydell and Everingham (1994) compare supply-control drug strategies (e.g. drug seizures) to demand-control strategies (e.g. drug treatment). Although comparing completely different programs, Rydell and Everingham were able to place these two approaches on an equal footing by estimating the reduced cocaine consumption from each alternative. They found a 1 percent reduction in cocaine consumption could be obtained by either spending $34 million on treatment or $246 million on domestic drug enforcement (Rydell and Everingham, 1994: 24, Table 3.2). This study is often cited as providing evidence that treatment is seven times more cost-effective than drug control programs.

Some analysts ask questions such as "what is the cost per offender?" without determining whether or not the program itself is effective. Although important, this is purely a "cost" analysis and should not be construed as a "cost-effectiveness" study. In order to be a cost-effectiveness study, one must measure outcomes (e.g. crimes averted, recidivism rate), not just inputs (e.g. number of offenders admitted to the program). More importantly, to focus solely on costs can easily result in a conclusion to fund a program even if it has few benefits.

Outside of crime, cost-effectiveness analysis has been applied in many different scenarios. For example, a myriad of government programs reduce the risk of death from consumer and motor vehicle products, highway and workplace accidents, medical care, etc. Tengs *et al.* (1995) calculated the "cost per life year save" from over 500 such programs. Although the median program cost $42,000 per life year saved, Tengs *et al.* (1995) report a wide range of interventions, from the best that save more resources than they cost, to the worst that cost as much as $10 billion per life year. Thus, without necessarily determining what the appropriate "value of a life" should be and withouth conducting a benefit–cost analysis, shifting resources between programs could save a greater number of life years at a lower cost.

## Benefit–cost studies

Although cost-effectiveness may be a useful tool for decisionmakers, it is not always adequate. As discussed above, even though Greenwood *et al.* (1996) were able to show which youth intervention program gave you the most "bang for your buck," we still do not know if any or all of these programs produce benefits that exceed their costs. Thus cost-effectiveness does not solve the more fundamental problem of whether any one program should be implemented. Perhaps the benefits of all programs exceed their costs—or perhaps none of them do.

Cost-effectiveness is even less worthwhile when comparing two programs that do not have common benefit metrics. Thus, for example, the Rydell and Everingham (1994) study discussed above was able to compare two different programs because they each resulted in the benefit of decreased cocaine consumption. Both programs were on an equal footing and could be compared on the basis of "dollars per unit of cocaine consumption reduced." But what if one program reduced cocaine while the other decreased home burglaries? How would you compare 100 grams of cocaine to one home burglary?

Only by fully monetizing the benefits of crime reduction can these questions be answered. To date, only a few researchers have gone beyond cost-effectiveness analysis to explicitly compare the monetary costs to the monetary value of benefits. The fact that there have been few such studies to date is not surprising, given the fact that researchers involved in criminal justice program evaluation are seldom economists, and are not necessarily trained to analyze costs and benefits. In addition, until recently, no credible monetary estimates existed for intangible costs of crime. Moreover, introducing a new metric such as intangible costs takes a considerable amount of time before it becomes "mainstream" in a literature. As discussed in Chapter 2, the approach is not without controversy.

Among the authors who have used monetary estimates of the cost of crime (including intangible costs) in conducting benefit–cost analyses are DiIulio and Piehl (1991), Gray (1994), Levitt (1996), and Donohue and Siegelman (1998). Among the programs studied by these authors are longer prison sentences, prison overcrowding, rehabilitation programs, and juvenile intervention programs. Welsh and Farrington (1999) contains a summary of recent studies that measure costs and benefits of crime prevention programs, as well as a discussion of some of the methodological issues surrounding benefit–cost analysis. McDougall *et al.* (2003) contains a systematic review of all benefit–cost analyses of sentencing policies and finds only nine studies that provide adequate information to prepare such an analysis—many of which were also contained in the Welsh and Farrington (1999) review article.

Benefit–cost analysis is often more of an art than a science. One of the main areas of subjectivity is in the benefits measure that is chosen. Most of the discussion focuses on whether to include private versus social costs and whether or not to monetize intangible costs. While economists think of benefit–cost analysis from the perspective of "social costs," not all studies start from that perspective. Some studies have looked exclusively at the costs and benefits to taxpayers—which ignores the huge intangible costs to victims. Even if the study focuses on "social costs" instead of "taxpayer costs," as discussed in Chapter 2, there is not 100 percent agreement even among economists about which costs should be considered social costs in the context of crime. Recall, for example, the question of whether property theft should be considered a "social cost" if it is essentially a transfer of property from one person (victim) to another (offender). Similarly, different opinions exist about the validity of including the lost productivity of offenders who are incarcerated as a "cost" of incarceration.

Another important choice that needs to be made when conducting a benefit–cost analysis is which costs and benefits are incremental to the decision being made. From an economics perspective, only the costs (and benefits) that vary with the decision should be considered. However, implementing this rule is often less than straightforward, and requires a careful analysis of which costs and benefits vary with the decisions. For example, suppose a local court is considering whether to establish a new drug rehabilitation program that will divert first-time non-violent offenders as an alternative to incarceration. In that case, the policy analyst might want to compare the average cost of drug treatment to the alternatives, since both fixed and incremental costs will vary with the decision about whether or not to start up this program. Suppose the alternative is incarceration for those offenders, and there is adequate prison space available. In that case, we would compare the average cost of the drug treatment program to the incremental cost of incarceration. Since there are plenty of prison beds available, the fixed costs associated with prison construction and maintenance do not vary with our decision about whether or not to institute this drug treatment program. Hence the fixed costs of incarceration are irrelevant in this case. Of course, this may not be true if the alternative to a drug treatment program is to build a new prison. Similarly, in some instances, average costs are irrelevant. For example, suppose a drug rehabilitation program is already operational, and there is excess physical capacity. In this case, the only relevant costs to the decision whether or not to expand the program are the incremental costs of adding program participants.

In some cases, conducting a benefit–cost analysis is relatively easy because the benefits clearly outweigh the costs even ignoring benefits that are difficult to quantify. Thus, in cases where a program passes a benefit–cost test using just tangible costs, the need for monetizing intangible losses is less obvious. For example, Prentky and Burgess (1990) show the cost of incarcerated sex offender treatment is less than tangible benefits from lower recidivism rates (e.g. lower reprocessing costs of recidivists and lower victim costs). Prentky and Burgess did not need to estimate intangible benefits since the program already passes a benefit–cost test.

In order to understand the potential value—and pitfalls—of benefit–cost analysis, I next consider four examples of attempts to apply this technique in the criminal justice arena. These examples illustrate how this method can be applied to a wide variety of programs, including corrections, prevention, rehabilitation, and situational crime prevention.

### Corrections example: Illinois early release

Austin (1986) conducted a detailed study of the Illinois early-release program and its impact on recidivism and costs. He found that the reduced prison costs (i.e. savings to taxpayers) more than offset the cost associated with the slight increase in crimes committed by recidivists. In order to make that judgment, however, one must have a reasonable estimate of both the cost savings from early release and the cost increase owing to recidivism. At the time, the only crime-specific estimates of crime costs were based on out-of-pocket losses to crime victims. Austin (1986) used those out-of-pocket crime cost estimates in his benefit–cost analysis. Thus the cost of a rape was assumed to be only about $350 in his study. Cohen (1988a) reestimated the benefit–cost ratios using dollar estimates of the non-monetary costs of crime in addition to out-of-pocket costs. At the time, Cohen (1988a) estimated the cost of a rape, for example, to be over $51,000 in 1985 dollars. Using these figures, Cohen (1988a) reached the opposite conclusion—that Illinois would have benefited from keeping those prisoners incarcerated and building more prisons rather than incur the additional costs associated with crimes committed by recidivists. To conclude that this early-release program was worthwhile is tantamount to balancing the state budget on the backs of crime victims.

It is important to keep in mind that both Austin (1986) and Cohen (1988a) were comparing only two options—early release or building new prisons. This can lead to inefficient solutions. Perhaps other viable options would have provided higher benefits and/or lower costs. For example, intermediate sanctions such as home detention or intensive probation for first-time non-violent offenders would have cost less than building new prisons. Thus a comprehensive analysis of alternatives would have been preferred to a simple comparison of two options. Indeed, a careful benefit–cost analysis should always consider all feasible alternatives.

### Prevention example: Perry preschool project

While the last example involved benefits and costs that accrue around the same period of time, many programs do not yield benefits until many years after the expenditures have already been incurred. Although this presents challenges in terms of measuring program benefits and comparing costs across time periods, they are not necessarily insurmountable. In one study, Barnett (1993) compared the costs and benefits of the Perry Preschool Study, a preschool intervention program that included a control group whose participants have been followed periodically through age 27. He concluded that

---

### Philosophical concerns about benefit–cost analysis

Kelman (1981) articulates several concerns over the use of benefit–cost analysis on ethical and philosophical grounds. He argues that some things simply cannot be valued, such as free speech, pollution, or safety.[5] He also argues that benefit–cost analysis assumes that economic efficiency is the goal—at the expense of other socially desirable goals such as equity or fairness. This is not a criticism of the methodology—only of those who want to impose benefit–cost analysis as the sole criterion for public decisionmaking. Benefit–cost analysis does not discriminate on the basis of socioeconomic status. A $1,000 medical cost is valued at $1,000 regardless of whether the person being injured is rich or poor. Thus the tool is politically neutral and can (and will) be overridden when other policy goals come into conflict. Instead, when viewed as one tool available to policymakers, benefit–cost analysis itself has many benefits and only limited costs. Indeed, most texts on benefit–cost methodology include an analysis of the "incidence" of costs and benefits—i.e. who bears the costs and who reaps the benefits—as an integral part of benefit–cost analysis. The policymaker is presented the evidence and left to determine how to weight the differing goals of economic efficiency and equity.

A more subtle concern is the fact that the methodology itself may incorporate inequities in society. For example, if one is measuring lost wages to victims of crime—and those victims tend to be in the lower income quartiles—the benefits of a crime prevention program will be skewed downward based on the victim's income. If one were to compare a crime reduction program to another program that targets airline safety, for example, the typical wage rate might be higher for the airline accident victim than the crime victim. Further, if one were to conduct a survey of potential victims to determine their willingness to pay for crime reduction programs, the value one elicits is likely to be highly dependent on the wealth (i.e. ability to pay) of the respondent. Thus, from a public policy standpoint, benefit–cost analysis does indeed discriminate against the less wealthy in society. If society deems this to be unfair, the analyst needs to make adjustments in the estimated costs and benefits to "neutralize" the effect of wealth on them. This has been done to some extent in some of the empirical studies of the cost of crime. For example, the methodology developed in Cohen (1988a) is based on the statistical "value of life" of the typical individual in the U.S.—not on the typical crime victim. However, wage losses and reported short-term medical costs are necessarily taken from crime victim surveys.

Benefit–cost analysis is only one tool that policymakers can use in analyzing whether or not to adopt a prevention or criminal justice program. No matter how careful the analysis there will always be uncertainties and areas that cannot be quantified. In addition, other concerns such as fairness or distributional consequences might outweigh any benefit–cost considerations in some cases. If so, at least we can determine how much we are paying for that non-economic goal of fairness.

the costs—about $12,000 per participant—were outweighed by the benefits—about $50,000 in present value terms. However, these benefits accrued over more than 20 years, and Barnett estimated that the program did not pay for itself until about 20 years. Programs with such long payback periods require legislators with a long-term perspective who are willing to invest today's tax dollars in exchange for a payback that might not accrue for many years—long after they have left public office.

### Rehabilitation example: drug treatment programs

Rajkumar and French (1997) compare the costs and benefits of drug treatment programs, where the benefits are estimated to be the monetary value of reduced crime committed by rehabilitated drug abusers. Based on the Treatment Outcome Prospective Study (TOPS) of 11,750 drug abusers, they compared the monetary value of reduced crime one year following treatment to the cost of the program. They concluded that the cost of treatment for one drug abuser was far outweighed by the benefit of reduced crime. A study of more recent drug treatment programs (U.S. Department of Health and Human Services, 1997) suggests there are other substantial benefits from treatment including reduced medical costs, increased employment, and reduced welfare benefits not accounted for in the crime control benefits estimated in Rajkumar and French (1997).

## Situational crime prevention

Some crime prevention programs are targeted at reducing the opportunity to commit crime as opposed to focusing on potential offenders themselves. An example of such "situational crime prevention" is improved street lighting. Painter and Farrington (2001) report on a benefit–cost analysis of improved street lighting in two cities in England. In a controlled experiment, street lighting was improved in certain areas and not in others. Crime was monitored in both areas over a one-year period. The added street lighting was estimated to reduce vehicle theft, vandalism, larceny, and burglary—by amounts ranging from 12 percent to 46 percent relative to the control areas. The cost of street lighting includes ongoing electricity, light bulbs, and maintenance, in addition to the cost of the light fixtures and installation. Of course, street lighting lasts for more than one year, and the capital costs of installing lighting can be amortized over a long time period in order to look at the annual costs of additional street lighting. Thus the appropriate comparison is between the annualized costs and benefits. Painter and Farrington found that the annual crime reduction benefits exceeded the annual costs of lighting by about 24 to 1 in one city and 54 to 1 in the other. These benefit–cost ratios are so high that these programs actually pay for themselves—including the capital costs—in one year or less.

## Comprehensive benefit–cost assessments

While there have only been a handful of benefit–cost analyses of criminal justice or crime prevention programs, there are hundreds of program evaluations that estimate program effectiveness. The Sherman *et al.* (1997) study included over 500 program evaluations. More have been conducted since then. Since it is likely to be many years before there are an adequate number of benefit–cost studies to draw many inferences, one very promising approach to evaluating the costs and benefits of programs is to use the existing effectiveness studies to infer costs and benefits. To date, the best example of this approach was prepared by Steve Aos and his colleagues at the Washington State Institute for Public Policy (WSIPP) (Aos *et al.*, 2001). WSIPP was mandated by the Washington State legislature to "evaluate the costs and benefits of certain criminal justice policies, violence prevention programs, and other efforts to decrease the criminal recidivism of juvenile and adult offenders, and certain at-risk behaviors of youth" (Aos *et al.*, 2001: 1). As a result, they conducted an extensive benefit–cost analysis of programs designed to reduce crime—including programs targeted toward early childhood education, youth, juvenile offenders, and adult offenders. Not only is this a comprehensive and thorough study of costs and benefits, it is also unique in that there is a consistent and transparent methodology throughout the study. Thus it is possible to compare programs that are vastly different in their target population and crime reduction goals.

The approach taken by Aos and his colleagues was to first conduct a meta-analysis of "effectiveness" studies of various crime reduction programs. A "meta-analysis" is a systematic approach to examine existing studies. Thus it treats each existing study as a single observation and identifies all of the key features of the study. Thus the Aos *et al.* (2001) meta-analysis took into account the methodological rigor with which each study was conducted, using lower-end estimates of effectiveness and discounting studies that were not rigorous. Based on their analysis of all studies evaluating a particular intervention, they estimated the average "effect size"—the number of crimes averted per treated offender.

As Aos *et al.* (2001) note, most program evaluations cover only a small time period—oftentimes six months to one year. Yet we expect program benefits to continue throughout a criminal career—if only at a somewhat reduced rate. Thus the number of crimes averted is not taken directly from the underlying studies. Instead it is based on a criminal career model for offenders in the state of Washington. If a program reports on the first six months of reduced offending, Aos *et al.* (2001) might then infer a reduced offending rate that stretches out over the criminal career. This is not a simple process, and is based on a considerable amount of modeling and regression analysis. The end result is an estimate of the number of crimes averted per program participant per year—over the lifetime of the criminal offender. This is the "benefit" of the program.

This "benefit" of the program was then translated into dollar values. Aos *et al.* (2001) provide two estimates of monetary benefits—the first is based on taxpayer benefits and the second includes the benefit to potential crime victims. Since they use the monetary estimates from Miller, Cohen, and Wiersema (1996) to estimate the cost of crime to victims, these estimates include pain, suffering, and reduced quality of life. Since averted crimes are spread out over a number of years, the monetary benefits are discounted to present value at a real discount rate of 3 percent.

The benefits tallied up in the Aos *et al.* (2001) study only include crime reductions. They do not include many potential benefits such as increased educational outcomes, reduced teen pregnancy, reduced substance abuse, or other social benefits. Thus the benefits of some of these programs might be considerably higher. Like most attempts at a meta-analysis and/or comprehensive benefit–cost study, this approach has other limitations. For example, the estimated annual crime reductions are based on recidivism rates in the state of Washington, yet the underlying effectiveness rates are based on nationwide data—or data from particular states in which the underlying study is based. To the extent that recidivism rates in Washington are higher or lower than elsewhere, benefits of crime reduction programs would be correspondingly higher or lower.

Table 5.1 summarizes the results of the Aos *et al.* (2001) study for adult offender programs. They evaluate numerous drug treatment programs—both in and out of a prison setting. In a prison setting with community

*Table 5.1* Cost–benefit ratios for adult offender programs analyzed by Washington State Institute for Public Policy

| Program | Cost per participant ($) | Taxpayer benefit ($) | Taxpayer and crime victim benefit ($) | Benefit to cost ratios |
|---|---|---|---|---|
| *Drug treatment programs* (compared to no treatment): In-prison therapeutic community with community aftercare | 2,604 | (243) | 5,230 | 0.9 to 3.0 |
| Non-prison therapeutic community (in addition to residential facility) | 2,013 | 4,110 | 15,836 | 3.0 to 8.9 |
| Drug courts | 2,562 | (109) | 4,691 | 0.5 to 1.6 |
| Case management substance abuse programs | 2,204 | (1,050) | 1,230 | 0.5 to 1.6 |
| Community-based substance abuse treatment | 2,198 | 237 | 5,048 | 1.1 to 3.3 |
| *Intermediate sanctions* Intensive supervision (vs. probation or parole) | 3,296 | (2,250) | (384) | 0.3 to 0.9 |
| Treatment-oriented intensive supervision (vs. probation or parole) | 3,811 | (459) | 5,520 | 0.9 to 2.4 |
| Intensive supervision (vs. incarceration) | (5,925) | 6,083 | 6,386 | * |
| Boot camps (vs. incarceration) | (9,725) | 9,822 | 10,011 | * |
| *Other programs* Work release (vs. incarceration) | 456 | 507 | 2,351 | 1.1 to 5.2 |
| Job counseling/search for inmates leaving prison | 772 | 625 | 3,300 | 2.2 to 5.3 |

Note: All figures in 2000 dollars and taken from Aos *et al.* (2001).

*These programs save money without statistically significant changes in crime.

aftercare, they find that the added cost of the program is not quite offset by the reduced taxpayer costs associated with lower recidivism. Thus the benefit–cost ratio is only 0.9 considering taxpayer benefits. That is, for every dollar of taxpayer costs, 90 cents of benefits are received. However, including victim benefits, the results are dramatically different, with a benefit–cost ratio of three to one (three dollars of benefits for every dollar spent). For offenders in a residential setting, adding a similar program has a very high benefit–cost ratio, ranging from three to 8.9 to one. Drug courts have been shown to be effective at reducing recidivism. However, like in-prison treatment programs, they only pass a benefit–cost test if crime victim benefits are considered.

Aos *et al.* (2001) also examined several forms of intermediate sanctions such as intensive supervision and boot camps. They do not find much support for intensive supervision compared to more standard probation or parole, with benefit–cost ratios of less than one even when victim benefits are considered. However, when coupled with some form of intensive treatment for the offender, that result changes. For example, offering treatment-oriented intensive supervision results in a benefit–cost ratio of 2.4 to one when crime victim benefits are included. When compared to incarceration, however, intensive supervision is not only less costly, but recidivism rates are no higher; hence, for the type of offender normally found in such programs, they have been found to be cost-beneficial. Similar results are found for boot camps (relative to incarceration).

Finally, Aos *et al.* (2001) also report on several employment-related programs—including work-release and job counseling or search assistance following release from incarceration. Both of these programs have positive benefit–cost ratios.

Table 5.2 summarizes the results of the Aos *et al.* (2001) study for juvenile offender programs. Numerous "off-the-shelf" programs that are commonly used in Washington State have been found to pass a benefit–cost test, including "multi-systemic therapy," "functional family therapy," "aggression replacement training," "multidimensional treatment for foster care," and the "adolescent diversion project." These programs generally involve some form of intensive community-based intervention that might include the schools and/or the juvenile offender's family. As Aos *et al* (2001: 17) note, "The economics of these programs are generally the most attractive of any programs we reviewed in our entire cost–benefit analysis." In all cases, the benefit–cost ratios were at least 7 to 12 (using just taxpayer benefits) and as much as 25 to 45 (including victim benefits).

Like adult offenders, intensive supervision for juveniles is found to be a good alternative to incarceration. Similarly, intensive probation for juvenile offenders was found to be just barely cost-beneficial from a taxpayer standpoint. It becomes more beneficial when victim benefits are considered. One program—"scared straight"—was found to be ineffective at reducing crime and hence would never pass a benefit–cost test unless it was substituting for another more costly program.

The largest benefit–cost ratio was generally found in programs targeting juvenile offenders. For example, an aggression replacement training program was estimated to pay taxpayers $738 per program participant, and reduce crime by 18 percent. The benefits to taxpayers are estimated to be $8,287—more than $11 for every dollar spent. When victim benefits are included, these programs were estimated to pay back $33,143—about $45

*Table 5.2* Cost–benefit ratios for juvenile offender programs analyzed by Washington State Institute for Public Policy

| Program | Cost per participant ($) | Taxpayer benefit ($) | Taxpayer and crime victim benefit ($) | Benefit to cost ratios |
|---|---|---|---|---|
| *"Off-the-shelf" programs* | | | | |
| Multi-systemic therapy | 4,743 | 31,661 | 131,918 | 7.7 to 28.8 |
| Functional family therapy | 2,161 | 14,149 | 59,067 | 7.5 to 28.3 |
| Aggression replacement training | 738 | 8,287 | 33,143 | 12.2 to 45.9 |
| Multidimensional treatment foster care | 2,052 | 21,836 | 87,622 | 11.6 to 43.7 |
| Adolescent diversion project | 1,138 | 5,720 | 27,212 | 6.0 to 24.9 |
| *General treatment programs* | | | | |
| Diversion with services (vs. regular juvenile court processing) | (127) | 1,470 | 5,679 | * |
| Intensive probation (vs. regular probation) | 2,234 | 176 | 6,812 | 1.1 to 4.0 |
| Intensive probation (vs. incarceration) | (18,478) | 18,586 | 18,854 | * |
| Intensive parole (vs. regular parole) | 2,635 | (117) | 6,128 | 0.9 to 3.3 |
| Coordinated services | 603 | 3,131 | 14,831 | 6.2 to 25.6 |
| "Scared straight"-type programs | 51 | (6,572) | (24,531) | – |
| Family-based therapy | 1,537 | 7,113 | 30,936 | 5.6 to 21.1 |
| Juvenile sex offender treatment | 9,920 | (3,119) | 23,602 | 0.7 to 2.4 |
| Juvenile boot camps (vs. incarceration) | (15,424) | 10,360 | (3,587) | 3.04 to 0.81** |

Note: All figures in 2000 dollars and taken from Aos *et al.* (2001).

* These programs save money without significant changes in crime.

– These programs cost money without any significant changes in crime (or with an increase in crime).

** While juvenile boot camps result in lower costs than incarceration, they also result in higher criminal justice-related and victim costs owing to higher recidivism. Thus, unlike the other programs, including "victim benefits" in the cost–benefit analysis actually reduces the net benefits of the program. In this case, juvenile boot camps save the government/taxpayer money and have a benefit–cost ratio of 3 to 1. However, this comes at the expense of crime victims. Overall, including crime victims, the benefit–cost ratio is less than one.

per dollar spent. Other programs not shown in Table 5.2 were also analyzed, including some early childhood education programs such as nurse home visitation and early child preschool programs. Some of these have been found to be cost-beneficial. Thus shifting government resources away from programs that cost more than they deliver and into those that have been proven cost-beneficial could have major long-term social benefits.

## Monetary value of saving a high-risk youth

A somewhat different approach to benefit–cost analysis was taken by Cohen (1998), in which was asked the generic question, "what is the monetary value of saving a high-risk youth from a life of crime, drug abuse, or dropping out of high school?" This question is "generic" because it is not tied to any one particular crime prevention program. Instead, it looks at aggregate data on the frequency with which a juvenile delinquent and a career criminal commit crimes over their lifespan. For example, it is estimated that the typical career criminal commits three assaults, 1.25 robberies, 1.25 burglaries, 2.5 larcenies, 2.5 motor vehicle thefts, and 0.1 rapes per year. As shown in Table 5.3, the typical robbery, for example, was estimated to impose $2,700 in tangible costs, $6,700 in intangible costs, and $6,200 in the risk of death. Thus the total cost per robbery is $15,600. Since the average career criminal engages in 1.25 robberies per year, the annual cost of robbery for a career criminal is $19,500 (1.25 × $15,600). Similar calculations are done for the other crimes. In all, the 10.6 crimes committed per year by the average career criminal cost victims $165,000 per year in both tangible and intangible costs.

The typical "career" lasts six years, but the average offender also spends 8 years in jail or prison. Based on the probability of a career criminal being arrested and incarcerated, one can also estimate the annual cost to the

*Table 5.3* The annual cost to victims of a career criminal (1997 dollars)

| Crime | Tangible ($) | Intangible ($) | Risk of death ($) | Total per crime ($) | No. per year | Total per year |
|---|---|---|---|---|---|---|
| Rape | 6,000 | 96,000 | 1,000 | 103,000 | 0.1 | 10,300 |
| Robbery | 2,700 | 6,700 | 6,200 | 15,600 | 1.25 | 19,500 |
| Agg. assault | 1,800 | 9,200 | 29,700 | 40,700 | 3.0 | 122,100 |
| Burglary | 1,300 | 350 | – | 1,650 | 1.25 | 2,065 |
| Larceny | 440 | 0 | – | 440 | 2.5 | 1,000 |
| MV theft | 4,100 | 350 | – | 4,500 | 2.5 | 11,200 |
| Total | | | | | 10.6 | 165,000 |

Source: Cohen (1998).

Note: Numbers may not add owing to rounding.

Table 5.4 The lifetime costs of a career criminal (1997 dollars)

| Cost category | Total costs ($) | Present value (2% discount rate) ($) |
| --- | --- | --- |
| *Juvenile career* | | |
| Victim costs | 62,000–250,000 | 60,000–244,000 |
| Criminal justice-related | 21,000–84,000 | 20,000–82,000 |
| *Subtotal* | *83,000–335,000* | *80,000–325,000* |
| *Adult career* | | |
| Victim costs | 1,000,000 | 850,000 |
| Criminal justice-related | 335,000 | 283,000 |
| Offender productivity | 64,000 | 54,000 |
| *Subtotal* | *1,400,000* | *1,200,000* |
| Total | *1.5–1.8 million* | *1.3–1.5 million* |

Source: Cohen (1998).

criminal justice system that is associated with that career. This is estimated to be $40,000 annually.

Each component of the "typical" offender's career is similarly evaluated and costs are assessed. Thus the victimization costs of individual crimes are added to the criminal justice costs, plus forgone earnings of the criminal while they are in prison, to arrive at an estimate of the costs imposed by each career criminal. As shown in Table 5.4, this approach resulted in an estimate of the value of saving one "high-risk" youth from a life of crime to be $1.3 to $1.5 million in 1997 dollars (discounted to present value). A recent study of 500 career criminals from an urban prison in one western state in the U.S. found a similar cost of $1.14 million in 2002 dollars (Delisi and Gatling, 2003). Comparable estimates in Cohen (1998) are $370,000 to $970,000 for a heavy drug abuser and $243,000 to $388,000 for a high-school dropout. Combining these three different costs (but eliminating overlap since some drug crimes would otherwise be counted twice) resulted in an estimate of the present monetary value of saving a high-risk youth of $1.7 to $2.3 million. As explained elsewhere in this book, one cannot simply "inflate" these numbers to current dollars because they are based on the best available data at the time in terms of the number of crimes, severity of crimes, etc. For example, if the typical assault is now more severe, costs will have increased by more than inflation, while if the typical criminal career is now shorter (owing to perhaps longer prison sentences to those who are caught), the cost of a criminal career may be lower. Nevertheless, as a first approximation, these numbers would be close to $2.0 to $2.7 million in 2004 dollars.

This methodology provides estimates of the benefit of saving a high-risk youth—irrespective of the program that is being evaluated. Thus it provides only one side of the equation, and provides a basis for others who want to conduct a benefit–cost analysis of their programs. If one has an estimate of the number of high-risk youth that are likely to be "saved" from a life of crime, a benefit–cost analysis becomes relatively straightforward. However, even absent such information, one might be able to ask the simple question of "how many youth in my program do I have to 'save' from a life of crime before the program becomes cost-beneficial?" In many cases, given the high cost of a "high-risk youth," programs will be deemed worthy of trial even without solid evidence.

Although the methodology for arriving at the monetary value of saving a high-risk youth is generally sound, caution must be used if researchers want to rely upon the actual dollar estimates that Cohen (1998) derived. To use these estimates, one must assume that the program being evaluated will actually prevent a certain number of high-risk youth from becoming "typical career criminals." If a program evaluator has longitudinal data assessing actual program participants, using those data would obviously be better than assuming a typical career criminal.

## Concluding remarks

We started this book out discussing the tragic shootings at Columbine High School. As I stated from the outset, many would argue that no amount of money would be adequate to compensate the victims or their families for this loss. I hope the reader now realizes that I agree with this statement. No amount of money can bring back a loved one or fully compensate them for their loss. Yet it does not follow that attempts to understand and fully quantify the monetary value of losses—and, more importantly, quantify society's willingness to pay to avoid such a tragedy—are without merit. The "cost of crime" is nothing more than the "benefit of reducing crime." Thus, in Chapter 4, when I argued the "cost" of a rape is $237,000, what I am really saying is that society would be willing to spend up to this amount to prevent one rape from occurring. If you have read this book carefully, you would realize that I do not mean the cost of a rape to any one person can be quantified and put in these terms. I would certainly not give up my life for $9.7 million—neither would I consent to my daughter's rape for $237,000. Instead, these numbers tell us how much society is willing to spend to prevent one rape from occurring—where a social program (whether it be prevention or incarceration) will statistically prevent some of these crimes from occurring. These are important numbers to have in a society where resources are scarce and where programs—whether they are social welfare programs, more police on the street, prevention programs for high-risk youth, new roads, or public arts—will always be competing for taxpayer dollars.

# Notes

## 1 Introduction and overview

1 As discussed in Chapter 2, there are methods that can be adopted to deal with the effect of wage inequality on estimating the cost of crime. In short, the analyst might adopt "average" wage rates in the U.S. in estimating the cost of lost wages. This puts all crime victims on an equal footing—regardless of their wealth.

2 As some critics have noted, all cost estimates are subject to considerable uncertainty and categories of cost will inevitably be left unaccounted for (Zimring and Hawkins, 1995). Thus, unless methods and assumptions are relatively consistent, or the unaccounted costs are known to be relatively small, any such comparisons are likely to be of questionable value.

3 Chapter 5 contains a more detailed discussion of benefit–cost analysis.

4 See Sherman *et al.* (1997) for a comprehensive examination of the effectiveness of alternative programs.

5 It is also an *ex post* measure that presumably is higher than the *ex ante* willingness to pay. We will discuss this further in Chapter 2.

## 2 An economic approach to crime and costing methodologies

1 French, Rachal, and Hubbard (1991) contains a useful discussion of the distinction between private, social, and external costs.

2 Chapters 8 and 9 of Hellman (1980) provide a useful discussion of the economics of victimless crimes.

3 More specifically, we would want to compare the rate of moving by individuals in a similar demographic group to that of the victim. For example, if retirement-age people tend to move frequently, we would want to compare their background rate of moving to that of retirement-age victims to see if the latter move more frequently.

4 On the other hand, it may not be possible to replicate a small pilot intervention program on a large enough scale to make a significant dent in aggregate crime rates. Replication may not be possible if the success of a program can partly be explained by the high level of commitment and intensity of interest by initial program participants, for example.

5 For illnesses that are essentially acute (i.e. less than one year's duration), incidence- and prevalence-based cost estimates will be roughly the same. Prevalence-based estimates are substantially higher for serious injuries (Miller and Luchter, 1988).

6 The concept of "present value" is fundamental to economics and is relatively easy to understand. A dollar today is worth more than a dollar tomorrow in purchasing power owing to inflation. Similarly, a dollar next year is worth less than

having a dollar today, since I could just as easily take that dollar and invest it at current interest rates and have more than a dollar next year. Thus when economists talk about the "present value" of a future income stream, they are simply computing the amount of money today that would be the equivalent to the amount needed in future years, after accounting for the fact that (a) prices and wages increase over time, and (b) today's dollars can be invested and interest compounded. Except in rare circumstances, present value is always less than future value.

7 Note that these are "net" discount rates, as they already account for inflation. Thus, for example, a 2 percent discount rate would be consistent with long-term cost of living increases of 4 percent and long-term interest rates of 6 percent.

8 Regardless of the theoretical concerns, Cohen (1990) finds that the jury award method yields estimates of the cost of an index crime that are consistent with the property value studies. Cohen and Miller (2003) find that jury awards are consistent with the value of a life year implied by the "value-of-life" studies based on worker wage-rate differentials.

9 For an overview of the contingent valuation method, see Mitchell and Carson (1989). Smith (1996) compared the valuation from two different proposed environmental projects and found that citizens could make a clear distinction between the two projects.

## 3 Victim costs

1 Source: Bureau of Justice Statistics (2004a). Note that similar numbers are shown in Chapter 4 of this book. Table 4.4 includes $57.7 billion for police, $43.5 billion for corrections, and $21.6 billion for judicial and legal services for a total of $122.8 billion in 1997.

2 Source: U.S. Bureau of the Census, Public Education Finances, 2001; March 2003: Table 8. Available at http://www.census.gov/govs/school/01fullreport.pdf.

3 Unfortunately, the survey design generally does not allow us to assess the underlying cause of mental illness. For example, if women who are likely to be raped are also women who (absent the rape) are likely to suffer from mental illness (e.g. owing to family or marital problems), we may infer a causal connection that is actually due to some other confounding factor. This problem may be somewhat ameliorated in the Kilpatrick, Edmunds, and Seymour (1992) study, since the illness in question—PTSD—is generally associated with a traumatic event.

4 Much of this section is based on Chapter 15, "Restitution," in Office for Victims of Crime (1998).

5 See Victim and Witness Protection Act of 1982, Pub. L. no. 97–291, Sec. 4, 96 Stat. 1249 (codified at 18 U.S.C. Secs. 1512–15; Fed. R. Crim. P. 32), and Mandatory Victim Restitution Act, Title II of the Antiterrorism and Effective Death Penalty Act of 1996, Pub. L. no. 104–132 (1996), 18 U.S.C. 3663A (1996). Among other things, federal judges are required to order full restitution in criminal cases or state on the record their reasons for not doing so.

6 *Victims of Crime Act of 1984*, Pub. L. no. 104–235, codified at 42 U.S.C. 10601–5, 18 U.S.C. 3050 (1996). Much of this section is taken from Chapter 14, "Crime Victim Compensation," in Office for Victims of Crime (1998).

7 This approach is not necessarily followed in other countries. Instead, it is common to restrict payments to only monetary losses (as opposed to pain and suffering).

8 In 1985 there were approximately 911,000 tort filings in state and federal courts (Kakalik and Pace, 1986: 14). Assuming that 5 percent of these go to trial (Peterson and Priest, 1982), there would be about 45,500 cases going to trial in one

year. Thus JVR's 18,000 cases would represent about 40 percent of the verdicts in the U.S.

9  This progress has been due in large part to the legal research and advocacy efforts of the late Frank Carrington. A member of President Reagan's Task Force on Victims Rights, throughout the 1980s Mr. Carrington provided legal advice and advocacy to hundreds of crime victims. With support from the Office for Victims of Crime, he teamed up with the National Victim Center (NVC) in 1990 to create the nation's first training series on civil legal remedies for crime victims. Over the next several years, more than 2,000 victims, service providers, and attorneys were introduced to victims' rights through this nationwide training series. The NVC has carried on Mr. Carrington's work and compiled a database of over 9,000 case summaries of appellate court decisions relating to civil litigation by crime victims.

10  French, Rachal, and Hubbard (1991) provide a conceptual framework for estimating the costs of drug abuse.

11  See Caulkins (2000) for a discussion of the difficulty with measuring drug costs.

## 5  Policy analysis and the costs of crime

1  President Reagan promulgated the first such requirement in 1981, Executive Order 12291 (46 Federal Register 13193). In 1993 President Clinton issued Executive Order 12866 (58 Federal Register 51735). Although these Executive Orders cannot supercede statutory provisions, they have had a dramatic effect on the manner in which regulatory agencies draft and analyze proposed rules.

2  For example, see Senate Bill S. 981, 105th Congress (1997), which would require all major rules to be accompanied by a benefit–cost analysis.

3  Gramlich (1981) contains a historical overview of benefit–cost analysis as well as a textbook treatment of the fundamentals of this technique. See also Mishan (1988) for a standard textbook on benefit–cost analysis.

4  For example, see Oregon Senate Bill 267—"Evidence-Based Crime Prevention Programs" (2003), available at: http://www.ocjc.state.or.us/SB267/ESB267.pdf. The Oregon statute calls for an assessment of programs by September 2004. By July 2005, 25 percent of state funds must be spent on "evidence-based" programs or services. This figures increases to 50 percent by July 2007 and 75 percent by July 2009. Note that "evidence-based programs" must be based on scientific research and be "cost-effective," which means "cost savings realized over a reasonable period of time are greater than costs."

5  See Zerbe and Dively (1994: 263–70) for a detailed discussion of the Kelman article and opposing views in support of the use of benefit–cost analysis.

# References

Abt Associates, Inc. (1995). *What America's Users Spend on Illegal Drugs, 1988–93* (Spring).

Amick-McMullan, A., Kilpatrick, D.G., and Veronen, L.J. (1989). "Family Survivors of Homicide Victims: A Behavioral Analysis," *Behavior Therapist*. 12: 75–9.

Anderson, D.A. (1999). "The Aggregate Burden of Crime," *Journal of Law and Economics*. 42: 611–42.

Anonymous (1999). "Hundreds Mourn the Mother of Columbine Victim Who Killed Self," *Los Angeles Times* (October 28).

Aos, S., Phipps, P., Barnoski, R. and Lieb, R. (2001). *The Comparative Costs and Benefits of Programs to Reduce Crime*. Washington State Institute for Public Policy.

Arrow, K., Solow, R., Portney, P.R., Leamer, E.E., Radner, R., and Schuman, H. (1993). "Report of the NOAA Panel on Contingent Valuation." *Federal Register*. 58 (January 15, 1993): 4601–14.

Association of Certified Fraud Examiners (2002). *Report to the Nation on Occupational Fraud and Abuse.*

Austin, James (1986). "Using Early Release to Relieve Prison Crowding: A Dilemma in Public Policy," *Crime and Delinquency*. 32: 404–502.

Barnett, W.S. (1993). "Benefit–Cost Analysis of Preschool Education: Findings from a 25-Year Follow-Up," *American Journal of Orthopsychiatry*. 63: 500–8.

Bartley, W.A. (2000). "A Valuation of Specific Crime Rates," Ph.D. dissertation, Vanderbilt University.

Becker, G. (1968). "Crime and Punishment: An Economic Approach," *Journal of Political Economy*. 78: 169–217.

Black, D.J. (1998). *The Social Structure of Right and Wrong*. San Diego, CA: Academic Press.

Brand, S. and Price, R. (2001). *The Economic and Social Costs of Crime*. Home Office Research Study no. 217, available at: http://www.homeoffice.gov.uk/rds/pdfs/hors217.pdf.

Brantingham, P. and Easton, S.T. (1998). "The Costs of Crime: Who Pays and How Much? 1998 Update." The Fraser Institute, available at: http://www.fraserinstitute.ca/admin/books/files/CstsCrm1998.pdf.

Bureau of Justice Statistics (1989). "The Redesigned National Crime Survey: Selected New Data." NCJ 114746 (Washington, D.C.: U.S. Department of Justice).

—— (1993). "Survey of State Prison Inmates, 1991" (Washington, D.C.: U.S.

Department of Justice) NCJ 136949 (May). Available at: http://www.ojp.usdoj. gov/bjs/pub/pdf/sospi91.pdf.

—— (1994). "Elderly Crime Victims" (Washington, D.C.: U.S. Department of Justice) NCJ 147002 (March).

—— (1995). "Probation and Parole Violators in State Prison, 1991" (Washington, D.C.: U.S. Department of Justice) NCJ 149076 (August).

—— (1997). "1997 Justice Expenditure and Employment Extracts" (Washington, D.C.: U.S. Department of Justice). Available at: http://www.ojp.usdoj.gov/bjs/ pub/sheets/cjee97.zip.

—— (1998). "Profile of Jail Inmates, 1996." (Washington, D.C.: U.S. Department of Justice), NCJ 164620 (March). Available at: http://www.ojp.usdoj.gov/bjs/pub/ pdf/pji96.pdf.

—— (2002). *Sourcebook of Criminal Justice Statistics Online Edition*. Available at: http://www.albany.edu/sourcebook/.

—— (2003a). "Criminal Victimization, 2002" (Washington, D.C.: U.S. Department of Justice), NCJ 199994 (August). Available at: http://www.ojp.usdoj.gov/bjs/ pub/pdf/cv02.pdf.

—— (2003b). "State Court Sentencing of Convicted Felons, 2000: Statistical Tables" (Washington, D.C.: U.S. Department of Justice), NCJ 198822 (June). Available at: http://www.ojp.usdoj.gov/bjs/pub/pdf/scscf00.pdf.

—— (2003c). "Census of State and Federal Correctional Facilities, 2000" (Washington, D.C.: U.S. Department of Justice), NCJ 198272 (August). Available at: http://www.ojp.usdoj.gov/bjs/pub/pdf/csfcf00.pdf.

—— (2004a). "Expenditure and Employment Statistics" (Washington, D.C.: U.S. Department of Justice). Available at: http://www.ojp.usdoj.gov/bjs/eande.htm.

—— (2004b). "Crime and the Nation's Households, 2002" (Washington, D.C.: U.S. Department of Justice), NCJ 201797 (February). Available at: http://www.ojp. usdoj.gov/bjs/pub/pdf/cvus02.pdf.

Burt, M.R. and Katz, B.L. (1985). "Rape, Robbery, and Burglary: Responses to Actual and Feared Victimization, with Special Focus on Women and the Elderly," *Victimology: An International Journal*. 10: 325–58.

Burton, V.S. Jr., Cullen, F.T., and Travis, L.F., III. (1987). "The Collateral Consequences of a Felony Conviction: A National Study of State Statutes," *Federal Probation*. 51 (September): 55.

Butterfield, F. (1996). "Study Reveals High Cost of Crime in U.S.," *New York Times* (April 22).

Carrington, F. (1978). "Victims' Rights: A New Tort?," *Trial*. 14 (6): 39/59.

—— (1983). "Victims' Rights: A New Tort? Five Years Later," *Trial* 19 (12): 50–3.

Cart, J. (1999). "After Shootings, Calls for Help Flood Region," *Los Angeles Times* (May 11).

Caulkins, J.P. (2000). "Measurement and Analysis of Drug Problems and Drug Control Efforts," *Criminal Justice 2000*. National Institute of Justice, July 2000, NCJ 182411. Available at: http://www.ncjrs.org/criminal_justice2000/vol_4/04h. pdf.

Clotfelter, C.T. (1977). "Private Security and the Public Safety," *Journal of Urban Economics*. 5: 388–402.

Cohen, M.A. (1986). "The Costs and Benefits of Oil Spill Prevention and Enforcement," *Journal of Environmental Economics and Management*. 13: 167–88.

—— (1987). "Optimal Enforcement Strategy to Prevent Oil Spills: An Application of a Principal-Agent Model with 'Moral Hazard,'" *Journal of Law and Economics*. 30: 23–51.

—— (1988a). "Pain, Suffering, and Jury Awards: A study of the Cost of Crime to Victims," *Law and Society Review*. 22: 537–55.

—— (1988b). "Some New Evidence on the Seriousness of Crime," *Criminology*. 26: 343–53.

—— (1989). "Corporate Crime and Punishment: A Study of Social Harm and Sentencing Practice in the Federal Courts, 1984–1987," *American Criminal Law Review*. 26: 605–60.

—— (1990). "A Note on the Cost of Crime to Victims," *Urban Studies*. 27: 125–32.

—— (1998). "The Monetary Value of Saving a High Risk Youth," *Journal of Quantitative Criminology*. 14: 5–33.

—— (1999). "Alcohol, Drugs and Crime: Is 'Crime' Really One-Third of the Problem?," *Addiction* 94: 636–9.

—— (2000). "Measuring the Costs and Benefits of Crime and Justice," chapter (pp. 263–316 in Volume 4: "Measurement and Analysis of Crime and Justice") of *Criminal Justice 2000*. National Institute of Justice, July 2000, NCJ 182411. Available at: http://www.ncjrs.org/criminal_justice2000/vol_4/04f.pdf.

—— (2001). "The Crime Victim's Perspective in Cost–Benefit Analysis: The Importance of Monetizing Tangible and Intangible Crime Costs." Chapter 3 (pp. 23–50) in *Costs and Benefits of Preventing Crime*. David P. Farrington, Brandon C. Welsh, and Lawrence W. Sherman (eds). Boulder, CO: Westview Press.

Cohen, M.A. and Miller, T.R. (1998). "The Cost of Mental Health Care for Victims of Crime," *Journal of Interpersonal Violence*. 13: 93–100.

—— (2003). "'Willingness to Award' Nonmonetary Damages and the Implied Value of Life from Jury Awards," *International Review of Law and Economics*. 23: 165–81.

Cohen, M.A., Miller, T.R., and Rossman, S.B. (1993). "The Costs and Consequences of Violent Behavior in the United States," in J.A. Reiss, Jr. and J.A. Roth, eds, *Understanding and Preventing Violence: Consequences and Control of Violence*, vol. 4. Washington, D.C.: National Academy Press.

Cohen, M.A., Rust, R.T., Steen, S., and Tidd S. (2004). "Willingness-to-Pay for Crime Control Programs," *Criminology*. 42 (1): 86–106.

Cohen, M.A., Steen, S., and Rust, R.T. (2002). "Measuring Public Perception of Appropriate Prison Sentences." Report to National Institute of Justice, NCJ 199365. Available at: http://www.ncjrs.org/pdffiles1/nij/grants/199365.pdf.

Cook, P.J. (1983). "Costs of Crime," in S.H. Kadish, ed., *Encyclopedia of Crime and Justice*. New York: Free Press.

—— (1986). "The Demand and Supply of Criminal Opportunities," in M.H. Tonry and N. Morris, eds, *Crime and Justice: An Annual Review of Research*. Chicago: University of Chicago Press.

Cook, P.J. and Ludwig, J. (2000). *Gun Violence: The Real Costs*. New York: Oxford University Press.

Cook, P.J. and Zarkin, G.A. (1985). "Crime and the Business Cycle," *Journal of Legal Studies* 14: 115–28.

Council of Economic Advisors (2004). *Economic Report of the President, 2004*. Washington, D.C.: U.S. Government Printing Office. Available at: http://www.gpoaccess.gov/eop/index.html.

Cullen, F.T., Link, B.G., and Polanzi, C.W. (1982). "The Seriousness of Crime Revisited," *Criminology* 20: 83–102.

Delisi, M. and Gatling, J.M. (2003). "Who Pays for a Life of Crime? An Empirical Assessment of the Assorted Victimization Costs Posed by Career Criminals," *Criminal Justice Studies*. 16 (4): 283–93.

Demmert, H.G. (1979). "Crime and Crime Control: What are the Social Costs?" Technical Report CERDCR-3-79. Stanford University, Hoover Institution, Center for Econometric Studies of the Justice System.

DiIulio, J.J. and Piehl, A.M. (1991). "Does Prison Pay? The Stormy National Debate over the Cost-Effectiveness of Imprisonment," *Brookings Review* 28–35.

Donohue, J.T. and Siegelman, P. (1998). "Allocating Resources among Prisons and Social Programs in the Battle against Crime," *Journal of Legal Studies*. 27: 1–44.

Douglass, J.B., Kenney, G.M., and Miller, T.R. (1990). "Which Estimates of Household Production are Best?," *Journal of Forensic Economics* 4: 25–45.

Dugan, L. (1999). "The Effect of Criminal Victimization on a Household's Moving Decision," *Criminology*. 37: 903.

Federal Trade Commission (1998). *1995–1996 Report: Staff Summary of Federal Trade Commission Activities Affecting Older Americans*. Available at: http://www.ftc.gov/os/1998/9803/aging98.rpt.htm.

Frank, L.F. (1992). "The Collection of Restitution: An Often Overlooked Service to Crime Victims," *St. John's Journal of Legal Commentary*. 3: 107–34.

Freeman, R.B. (1996). "Why Do So Many Young American Men Commit Crimes and What Might We Do About It?," *Journal of Economic Perspectives*. 10: 25–42.

French, M.T., Rachal, J.V., and Hubbard, R.L. (1991). "Conceptual Framework for Estimating the Social Cost of Drug Abuse," *Journal of Health and Social Policy*. 2: 1–22.

Gaes, G.G. (1985). "The Effects of Overcrowding in Prison," in M.H. Tonry and N. Morris, eds, *Crime and Justice: An Annual Review of Research*. Chicago: University of Chicago Press.

Godfrey, C., Eaton, G., McDougall, C., and Culyer, A. (2002). *The Economic and Social Costs of Class A Drug Use in England and Wales, 2000*. Home Office Research Study no. 249, available at: http://www.homeoffice.gov.uk/rds/pdfs2/hors249.pdf.

Gold, M.R., ed. (1996). *Cost-Effectiveness in Health and Medicine*. New York: Oxford University Press.

Gramlich, E.M. (1981). *Benefit–Cost Analysis of Government Programs*. Englewood Cliffs, N.J.: Prentice-Hall.

Gray, C.M., ed. (1979). *The Costs of Crime*. Beverly Hills: Sage Publications.

Gray, T. (1994). "Research Note: Using Cost–Benefit Analysis to Measure Rehabilitation and Special Deterrence," *Journal of Criminal Justice*. 22: 569–75.

Greenwood, P.W., Model, K., Rydell, C.P., and Chiesa, J. (1996). *Diverting Children from a Life of Crime: Measuring Costs and Benefits*. Santa Monica, CA: Rand Corporation.

Greenwood, P.W., Rydell, C.P., Abrahamse, A.F., Caulkins, J.P., Chiesa, J., Model, K.E., and Klein, S.P. (1994). *Three Strikes and You're Out: Estimated Benefits and Costs of California's New Mandatory-Sentencing Law*. Santa Monica, CA: Rand Corporation.

Hartman, R. (1990). "One Thousand Points of Light Seeking a Number: A Case Study of CBO's Discount Rate Policy," *Journal of Environmental Economics and Management*. 18: S3–S7.

Hartunian, N.S., Smart, C.N., and Thompson, M. (1981). *The Incidence and Economics of Major Health Impairments: A Comparative Analysis of Cancer, Motor Vehicle Injuries, Coronary Heart Disease, and Strokes.* Lexington, MA: Lexington/Heath.

Haveman, R.H. and Wolfe, B.L. (1984). "Schooling and Economic Well-Being: The Role of Nonmarket Effects," *Journal of Human Resources.* 19: 377–407.

Hay, J.W. (1991). "The Harm They Do to Others: A Primer on the External Costs of Drug Abuse," in M.B. Krauss and E.P. Lazear, eds, *Searching for Alternatives: Drug-Control Policy in the United States* (Stanford, CA: Hoover Institution Press).

Hellman, D.A. (1980). *The Economics of Crime.* New York: St. Martin's Press.

Hellman, D.A. and Naroff, J.L. (1979). "The Impact of Crime on Urban Residential Property Values," *Urban Studies.* 16: 105–12.

Hoehn, J.P., Berger, M.C., and Blomquist, G.C. (1987). "A Hedonic Model of Interregional Wages, Rents, and Amenity Values," *Journal of Regional Science.* 27: 605–20.

Horowitz, M.J. (1986). "Stress-Response Syndromes: A Review of Posttraumatic and Adjustment Disorders," *Hospital and Community Psychiatry.* 37 (3): 241–9.

Insurance Information Institute (1996). *Insurance Issues Update* (September).

Irwin, J. and Austin, J. (1994). *It's About Time: America's Imprisonment Binge.* Belmont, CA: Wadsworth.

Jones, J.D., Jones, C.L., and Phillips-Patrick, F. (1994). "Estimating the Costs of the *Exxon Valdez* Oil Spill," *Research in Law and Economics.* 16: 109–50.

Kakalik, J.S. and Pace, N.M. (1986). *Costs and Compensation Paid in Tort Litigation.* Santa Monica, CA: Rand Corporation.

Kass, J. (1999). "Post-Littleton Bid to Revamp Schools: As Columbine High Begins Repairs, Nation Rethinks School Design," *Christian Science Monitor* (June 24).

Kelman, S. (1981). "Cost–Benefit Analysis—An Ethical Critique," *Regulation.* (January/February).

Kilpatrick, D.G., Edmunds, C., and Seymour, A. (1992). *Rape in America: A Report to the Nation.* Arlington, VA: National Center for Victims of Crime.

Kilpatrick, D.G., Resnick, H.S., and Amick, A. (1989). "Family Members of Homicide Victims: Search for Meaning and Post-Traumatic Stress Disorder." Paper Presented at the 97th Annual American Psychological Association Convention, New Orleans (August).

Kilpatrick, D. and Saunders, B. (1997). "Prevalence and Consequences of Child Victimization." Research preview, Washington, D.C.: National Institute of Justice (April).

Klaus, P.A. (1994). *The Costs of Crime to Victims.* Washington, D.C.: U.S. Department of Justice. NCJ 145865 (February).

Lehman, D.R., Wortman, C.B., and Williams, A.F. (1987). "Long-Term Effects of Losing a Spouse or Child in a Motor Vehicle Crash," *Journal of Personality and Social Psychology.* 52 (1): 218–31.

Levitt, S.D. (1996). "The Effect of Prison Population Size on Crime Rates: Evidence from Prison Overcrowding Litigation," *Quarterly Journal of Economics.* 319–51.

Lloyd, J. (1999). "Home Schooling's Latest Appeal: Safety," *Christian Science Monitor* (June 4).

LRP Publications (2001). *Personal Injury Valuation Handbook.* Horsham, PA: LRP Publications.

Ludwig, J. and Cook, P.J. (2001). "The Benefits of Reducing Gun Violence: Evidence from Contingent-Valuation Survey Data," *Journal of Risk and Uncertainty.* 22: 207–26.

McDougall, C., Cohen, M.A., Swaray, R. and Perry. A. (2003). "The Costs and Benefits of Sentencing—A Systematic Review," *Annals of the American Academy of Political and Social Science.* 587: 160–77 (May).

Macmillan, R. (2000). "Adolescent Victimization and Income Deficits in Adulthood: Rethinking the Costs of Criminal Violence from a Life-Course Perspective," *Criminology.* 38: 553.

Maltz, M.D. (1975). "Measures of Effectiveness for Crime Reduction Programs," *Operations Research.* 23: 452–74.

Martin, J.P. and Bradley, J. (1964). "Design of a Study of the Cost of Crime," *British Journal of Criminology.* 4: 591–603.

Mayhew, P. (2003). *Counting the Costs of Crime in Australia: Technical Report.* Australian Institute of Criminology Technical and Background Paper Series no. 4 (April). Available at: http://www.aic.gov.au/publications/tbp/tbp004.pdf.

Miczek, K.A., DeBold, J.F., Haney, M., Tidey, J., Vivian, J., and Weerts, E.M. (1994). "Alcohol, Drugs of Abuse, Aggression, and Violence." in A.J. Reiss, Jr. and J.A. Roth, eds, *Understanding and Preventing Violence: Social Influences*, vol. 3. Washington, D.C.: National Academy Press.

Miller, T.R. (1989). "Willingness to Pay Comes of Age: Will the System Survive?," *Northwestern University Law Review.* 83: 76–907.

Miller, T.R., Cohen, M.A., and Wiersema, B. (1996). "Victim Costs and Consequences: A New Look." National Institute of Justice Research Report, NCJ-155282. Available at: http://www.ncjrs.org/pdffiles/victcost.pdf.

Miller, T.R. and Luchter, L. (1988). "The Socioeconomic Impacts of Injuries Resulting from Motor Vehicle Crashes," in *Proceedings XXII FISITA Congress Technical Papers on Society of Automotive Engineers.* SAE P-211. Warrendale, PA: The Society: 2.513–2.527.

Mishan, E.J. (1988). *Cost–Benefit Analysis: An Informal Introduction*, 4th edition. London: Unwin Hyman.

Mitchell, R.C. and Carson, R.T. (1989). *Using Surveys to Value Public Goods.* Washington, DC: Resources for the Future.

Moore, M.J. and Viscusi, W.K. (1989). "Discounting Environmental Health Risks: New Evidence and Policy Implications," *Journal of Environmental Economics and Management.* 18: S51–S62.

National Association of Crime Victim Compensation Boards (2002). "Compensation for Crime Victims." Brochure available at: http://www.nacvcb.org/documents/BrochureCVC.pdf.

National Center for Victims of Crime (1997). *1996 Victims' Rights Sourcebook: A Compilation and Comparison of Victims Rights Laws*, Arlington, VA: National Victim Center. Available at: http://www.ncvc.org/resources/reports/sourcebook/.

National Institute of Drug Abuse (1992). *The Economic Costs of Alcohol and Drug Abuse in the United States—1992.* Available at: http://www.nida.nih.gov/EconomicCosts/Index.html.

—— (1999). "Research Shows Effects of Prenatal Cocaine Exposure Are Subtle But Significant," *NIDA Notes.* 14 (September). Available at: http://www.drugabuse.gov/NIDA_Notes/NNVol14N3/DirRepVol14N3.html.

National Institute of Justice (2004). *Solicitation for Criminal Justice Research.* Available at: http://www.ncjrs.org/pdffiles1/nij/sl000663.pdf (February).

Office of Management and Budget. (1992). "Guidelines and Discount Rates for Benefit–Cost Analysis of Federal Programs," *Federal Register*. 57: 53519 (November 10).

Office of National Drug Control Policy (2001). *The Economic Costs of Drug Abuse in the United States, 1992–1998*, publication no. NCJ-190636, Executive Office of the President, Washington, D.C. Available at: http://www.whitehousedrug policy.gov/publications/pdf/economic_costs98.pdf.

Office for Victims of Crime (1997). *Nation Wide Analysis, Victims of Crime Act, 1996 Victims of Crime Act Performance Report, State Compensation Program*. Washington, D.C.: U.S. Department of Justice, Office of Justice Programs, Office for Victims of Crime (April, 14).

—— (1998). *New Directions from the Field: Victims' Rights and Services for the 21st Century*. U.S. Department of Justice, NCJ 170600. Available at: http://www. ojp.usdoj.gov/ovc/new/directions/pdftxt/direct.pdf.

—— (2000). *Report to Congress, 1999*. Washington, D.C.: U.S. Department of Justice.

Palle, C. and Godefroy, T. (2000). "The Cost of Crime: A Monetary Assessment of Offending in 1996." Research on Crime and Criminal Justice in France: Penal Issues Newsletter March 2000. Available at: http://www.msh-paris.fr/cesdip/.

Painter, K.A. and Farrington, D.P. (2001). "The Financial Benefits of Improved Street Lighting Based on Crime Reduction," *Lighting Research and Technology*. 33: 3–10.

Petersilia, J. and Turner, S. (1986). *Prison Versus Probation in California: Implications for Crime and Offender Recidivism*. Santa Monica, CA: Rand Corporation.

Peterson, M.A. and Priest, G.L. (1982). *The Civil Jury: Trends in Trials and Verdicts, Cook County, Ill., 1960–1979*. Santa Monica, CA: Rand Corporation.

Phillips, L. and Votey, H.L., Jr. (1981). *The Economics of Crime Control*. Beverly Hills: Sage Publications.

Posner, R.A. (1980). *Economic Analysis of Law*. 2nd Edition. Boston, MA: Little Brown.

Prentky, R. and Burgess, A.W. (1990). "Rehabilitation of Child Molesters: A Cost–Benefit Analysis," *American Journal of Orthopsychiatry*. 60: 108–17.

Pynoos, R.S. and Eth, S. (1985). "Children Traumatized by Witnessing Acts of Personal Violence: Homicide, Rape, or Suicide Behavior," in S. Eth and R.S. Pynoos, eds, *Post-Traumatic Stress Disorder in Children*. Washington, D.C.: American Psychiatric Press.

Rajkumar, A.S. and French, M.T. (1997). "Drug Abuse, Crime Costs, and the Economic Benefits of Treatment," *Journal of Quantitative Criminology*. 13: 291–324.

Reuter European Business Report London (1996). "Music and Performer Groups Act to Curb Piracy" (September 26).

Reuter, P., MacCoun, R., and Murphy, P. (1990). *Money from Crime: A Study of the Economics of Drug Dealing in Washington, D.C.* Santa Monica, CA: Rand.

Revesz, R.L. (1999). "Environmental Regulation, Cost–benefit Analysis, and the Discounting of Human Lives," *Columbia Law Review*. 99: 941.

Richardson, R. (2003). *2003 CIS/FBI Computer Crime and Security Survey*. Computer Security Institute.

Rossi, P.H. and Berk, R.A. (1997). *Just Punishments: Federal Guidelines and Public Views Compared*. New York: De Gruyter.

Rossi, P.H., Waite, E., Boise, C.E., and Berk, R.A. (1974). "The Seriousness of Crimes: Normative Structure and Individual Differences," *American Sociological Review.* 39: 224–37.

Rydell, C.P. and Everingham, S.S. (1994). *Controlling Cocaine: Supply Versus Demand Programs.* Santa Monica, CA: Rand Corporation.

Samuels, C.A. (1999). "School Absenteeism Soars After Colorado Shootings," *Washington Post.* (May 1).

Sellin, T. and Wolfgang, M.E. (1966). *The Measurement of Delinquency.* New York: Wiley.

Serrano, R.A. and Moehringer, J.R. (1999). "Tragedy in Colorado: Thousands Embrace in Pledge to Mend Hearts," *Los Angeles Times* (April 26).

Sherman, L.W., Gottfredson, D., MacKenzie, D., Eck, J., Reuter, P., and Bushway, S. (1997). *Preventing Crime: What Works, What Doesn't, What's Promising.* Report to Congress. National Institute of Justice. NCJ-165366 (February).

Sherman, L.W. and Klein, J. (1984). *Major Lawsuits Over Crime and Security: Trends and Patterns, 1958–82.* College Park, MD: Institute of Criminal Justice and Criminology, University of Maryland.

Smith, B.E., Davis, R.C., and Hillenbrand, S.W. (1989). *Improving Enforcement of Court-Ordered Restitution: Executive Summary.* Chicago, IL: American Bar Association.

Smith, V.K. (1996). "Can Contingent Valuation Distinguish Economic Values for Different Public Goods?," *Land Economics.* 72: 139–51.

Streff, F.M., Molnar, L.J., Cohen, M.A., Miller, T.A., and Rossman, S.B. (1992). "Measuring Costs of Traffic Crashes and Crime: Tools for Informed Decision Making," *Journal of Public Health Policy.* 13: 451–71.

Tengs, T.O., Adams, M.E., Pliskin, J.S., Safran, D.G., Siegel, J.E., Weinstein, M.C., and Graham, J.D. (1995). "Five-Hundred Life-Saving Interventions and their Cost-Effectiveness," *Risk Analysis.* 15: 369–90.

Thaler, R. (1978). "A Note on the Value of Crime Control: Evidence from the Property Market," *Journal of Urban Economics.* 5: 137–45.

Titus, R.M., Heinzelmann, F., and Boyle, J.M. (1995). "Victimization of Persons by Fraud," *Crime and Delinquency.* 41: 54–72.

Trumbull, W.N. (1990). "Who Has Standing in Cost–Benefit Analysis?," *Journal of Policy Analysis and Management.* 9: 201–18.

United Nations Office on Drugs and Crime (1998). *Economic and Social Consequences of Drug Abuse and Illicit Trafficking.* Available at: http://www.unodc.org/pdf/technical_series_1998-01-01_1.pdf.

U.S. Department of Health and Human Services (1997). *National Treatment Improvement Evaluation Study (NTIES).* Available at: http://ncadi.samhsa.gov/govstudy/f027/.

U.S. General Accounting Office (1992). *Health Insurance: Vulnerable Payers Lose Billions to Fraud and Abuse* (May). Available at: http://161.203.164/t2pbat6/146547.pdf.

Viscusi, W.K. (1998). *Ra.tional Risk Policy.* Oxford: Clarendon Press.

—— (2000). "The Value of Life in Legal Contexts: Survey and Critique," *American Law and Economics Review.* 2: 195–222.

Washington, K. (1999). "Columbine Fund," *USA Today* (September 2).

Welsh, B.C. and Farrington, D.P. (1999). "Monetary Costs and Benefits of Crime

Prevention Programs," in M. Tonry, ed., *Crime and Justice: A Review of Research*. Chicago: University of Chicago Press.

Wilgoren, D. (1999). "Area Schools Enhancing Security: Shootings in U.S. Prompt New Policies," *Washington Post* (August 25).

Wirtz, P.W. and Harrell, A.V. (1987). "Assaultive Versus Nonassaultive Victimization: A Profile Analysis of Psychological Response," *Journal of Interpersonal Violence*. 2: 264–77.

Wolfgang, M.E., Figlio, R.M., Tracy, P.E., and Singer, S.I. (1985). *The National Survey of Crime Severity*. U.S. Dept. of Justice, Bureau of Justice Statistics.

Zarkin, G.A., Cates, S.C., and Bala, M.V. (2000). "Estimating the Willingness to Pay for Drug Abuse Treatment: A Pilot Study," *Journal of Substance Abuse Treatment*. 18: 149–59.

Zerbe, R.O., Jr., and Dively, D.D. (1994). *Benefit–Cost Analysis in Theory and Practice*. New York: HarperCollins.

Zimring, F.E. and Hawkins, G. (1995). *Incapacitation: Penal Confinement and the Restraint of Crime*. New York: Oxford University Press.

# Index

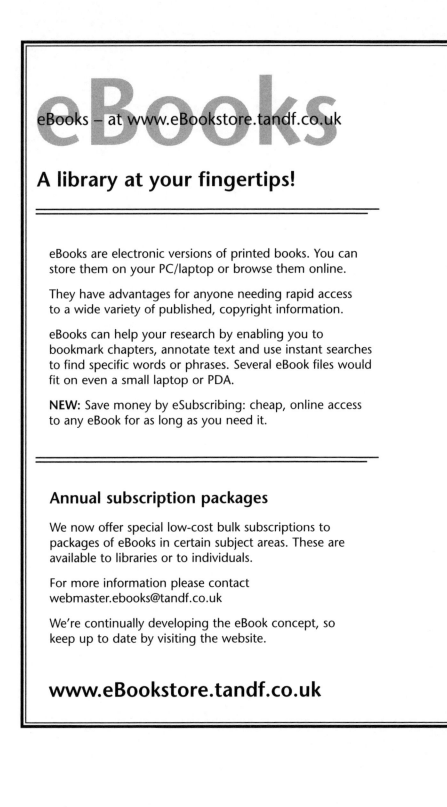